WHO MOVED MY STILTON ?

WHO MOVED MY STILTON ?

A GUIDE TO GETTING AHEAD IN BUSINESS

JEBEDIAH BLOOMSBURY
LONDON—PARIS—STOCKPORT

1896

CONTENTS

FOREWORD

By LADY CINDERELLA ROCKERFELLER, RAGS-TO-RICHES PUMPKIN MAGNATE & UPWARDLY MOBILE SIX-TIME WIDOW

WELCOME, DEAR READER, TO OUR LITTLE BOOK. For the man who wishes to hone his skills in the arts of management, negotiation, motivation and employee-enfearment, it is a simply indispensible companion.

I myself have been an indispensible companion to six very rich men, all of whom were some years older than myself and all of whom have sadly passed away. In the course of my tragic marriages, I have learned a great deal about the acquisition of wealth via trades as diverse as shipbuilding, property, haberdashery and certain earthier branches of the entertainment industry. All share many common characteristics, with the exception of property, where constant dishonesty is the only requisite attribute.

Since the regrettable dismantling of the feudal system, well-bred Englishmen have found commerce to be a rather vulgar *milieu*, but times are changing. Whether you have been defrocked by the Church, snubbed by the heiress of your choice, ejected from the Army for a quivering upper lip or simply born with an inadequately expansive country seat, there is no longer any shame in attempting to make your own money. Without further ado, let us get to it.

Cinders

CHAPTER 1

GETTING
AHEAD

BY SIR RODERICK 'ROCKY' RHODES
—

ADVENTURE CAPITALIST

I MAKE NO SECRET of the fact that I have made rather a lot of money, and I expect you would like to be able to say the same. I bagged my first fortune selling ice to the Eskimo peoples of the frozen North Pole, and then attempted to get my hands on an even greater sum by selling Eskimos to other Eskimos. Sadly, thanks to the meddling of various do-gooders, this lucrative trade has become difficult to conduct without unwelcome attention from the authorities, but the successful man of commerce does not worry too much about a little thing like the law, nor fuss about being chased for hundreds of miles across the tundra by irate Eskimo Abolitionists.

However, the experience was a painful and clear reminder that unless the City is allowed to do exactly as it pleases without the officious interference of government, morality &c., our great nation's status as a world economic leader will be lost forever.

I digress ; you of course wish to know about the specific methods and techniques that enabled me to build up a fortune from almost nothing (apart from a modest inheritance).

After my Arctic experience, I journeyed to Africa, where I formulated my theories of business from studying the wild animals habitant on that continent. These secrets I am delighted to share with you in this chapter. For a fuller insight into my methods, however, it is imperative that the would-be plutocrat attend one of my residential courses, details of which are elucidated on page 22 of this volume. I look forward to sharing my experiences with you, and confirm that cash, banker's draft or jewellery are all acceptable methods of payment.

Rocky

I AM TIGER—HEAR
MY ROAR !

BEING AN INSIGHT INTO THE MIND OF THE SUCCESSFUL
MAN OF BUSINESS AND AN EXPLANATION OF ALL THAT I
HAVE LEARNED IN MY TIME IN THE AFRICAN JUNGLE,
AND HOW IT CAN BE APPLIED TO THE COMMERCIAL
JUNGLE OF TODAY ...

IT WAS WHILE HUNTING TIGERS IN AFRICA that I
originated my first and most fundamental technique
for business accomplishment : *Release the Tiger Within—
and Shoot It in the Face.* It is my firm belief that each
and every one of us—no matter how poor, weak, dull
or Welsh—has a successful man, or "tiger", trapped
inside him. Via correct thought, decisive action and
strict adherence to my principles, this mighty beast
can be released.

Upon unleashing the tiger within, you will wonder how you ever stumbled along among the wretched herbivores upon whom we tigers prey. For we tigers are of a quite different essence to the unsuccessful *hoi polloi*. We are decisive. We are ruthless. Many of us are solitary hunters. Some of us have retractable claws. In short, like the tiger, we are to be feared.

Fig. 1. *Releasing the Tiger while Spanking the Monkey.*
For Advanced Capitalists only.

Of course, I am speaking metaphorically here. Only the most exceptional and extraordinarily wealthy have an actual large cat of the species *Panthera tigris* living within their person. One thinks immediately of the first Baron Rothschild, who was so fearsomely tigerish in everything he did that he would climb a tree each morning, pounce on an unsuspecting bison, devour it alive, and then run to his offices in King William Street, sometimes pausing en route to lick his own hindquarters. If you eat a live bison each morning, you will not go far wrong in commerce ; and it is my fervent hope that, in years to come, the streets of the City will be lined with wealthy Englishmen of commerce nibbling their own posteriors.

I am certain that the reader is now saying to himself : "I should very much like to be a tiger—but how ?" The best and surest ways include :

—REPEATING useful acronyms to yourself
—THINKING positively about all you undertake
—SHOUTING at your subordinates
—PLAYING at golf with people richer than yourself
—BEING BORN with an enormous fortune

Undertake some of these without delay, and your tiger will soon be released. If these fail, attend one of my reasonably priced INSTRUCTIONAL WORKSHOPS.

A note of caution. The successful man or "tiger" is a powerful creation and must be bent to your will, or else it will run riot through your entire existence, clawing the furniture, frightening the servants and making the keeping of deer in the grounds of your country seat quite impossible. In cases of an unruly inner tiger, you must shoot it with a blunderbuss and hang it on your wall.

Too often I see men release a tiger but fail to get it under control. Worse, we have seen financiers attempt to grab a tiger by the tail, precipitating commercial catastrophes from the South Sea Bubble to the fiasco in Brazil. One even hears reports of a CELTIC TIGER, a creature from across the Irish Sea that managed to get its paws on enormous sums of money in the form of loans from our more trusting neighbours on the Continent. The results, I need hardly add, were disastrous.

REMEMBER ALWAYS : the world of business in London is as dangerous and cut-throat as hunting animals in the jungle of Africa. Fortunately, London is less oppressively hot. The food, also, tends to be better, although one ought to avoid the Savoy on Mondays.

Fig. 2. Also to be avoided : Releasing your
Inner Tiger in a Bear Market.

SCEPTICS who do not subscribe to my methods—a wretched collection of individuals who are universally poor and unsuccessful, I might add—have challenged the veracity of the origins of my RELEASE THE TIGER dictum, arguing on the basis that there are no tigers in Africa. I give them all the same answer : "You are quite right. There are indeed no longer any tigers in Africa—*because I have shot them all.*" Visitors to my 150-room home in Sawbridgeworthfordbury-on-the-Naze derive considerable enjoyment from a tour of my pelt room, where I store some of the finest specimens. That I have personally shot over 4,000 tigers, and thus rid an entire continent of their stripy menace, is a source of enormous pride.

THE EFFICIENT MAN

IF I WERE TO SAY THE WORDS "energetic", "vigorous"
and "discipline" to you, dear reader, you would
naturally envision me bashing away lustily with the
polo mallet, licking a group of natives into shape in
preparation for a dangerous expedition into the jungle
or giving a slovenly waiter the pummelling of his life
around the back of a chophouse somewhere off Broad
Street.

Energy. Vigour. Discipline. These three admirable
qualities are of enormous help not just in the pursuit
of sporting enjoyment, acceptable table service or wild
animals, but in the pursuit of business excellence as well.

Men who have achieved great success have many
diverse characters, but they are without exception
EFFICIENT in all that they do. Efficiency is the great
driver of our age, and it is as wonderful an elixir as
any of those marvellous new cacao-derived embrocations
one rubs on to the nostrils to banish sluggish feelings.
When energy, vigour and discipline unite in a holy
trinity, efficiency is created. Harnessing its power is the
key to conquering commerce.

On a recent hunting expedition to Philadelphia—
where I managed to bag a splendid specimen of the
Ring Tailed, or 'Cheesesteak' Bear—I had the pleasure
of an audience with the wonderfully clever American
Mr Frederick Winslow Taylor. If I may be allowed
to indulge myself just this once in the sin of pride, I
must say that I take a deal of credit for inspiring Mr
Taylor in his researches into industrial efficiency, and
I am confident that many of the ideas I offered him
will go some way to leavening his writings on modern
production.

I. TIME IS HONEY

MY OWN STUDIES began in '83 while I was wintering in the Rift Valley. A local chief had given me a large swarm of African Killer Bees (*Stingus fatalis*) as a token of his appreciation, hiding them in the bottom of my hammock according to local custom. And while I was fortunate to receive many such gifts from grateful natives over the years—a man-eating crocodile in Borneo, a Black Widow in Bechuanaland, a rabid wolfhound in Great Missenden—it was the murderous frenzy of the humble Killer Bee which offered the most enlightening parallel to our own hives of commercial activity.

Fig. 1.
Droning on.

Although the swarm was fissiparous and inchoate to the casual observer, from my unique vantage point within it I perceived that each member of the hive was in fact moving in a deliberate and highly efficient way.

II. WTF ?

ARMED WITH ONLY A STOPWATCH and a box of bees
I was thus able to elaborate my first WORKING TIME
FORMULA (WTF) and so determine the optimal time
needed to perform a range of vital managerial tasks :

TASK	TIME
Smoking a cheroot	$3\frac{1}{2}$ *swarm*
Taking a nap after a long lunch	6 *swarm*
Breaking a strike among jute workers	*A-B+C swarm*
Pouring a glass of port	*Swarm^2/x^2-3*

Where A = Bee, B = Hay and C is constant room temperature.

The efficient apportionment of your working hours is
a boon in all aspects of industrial ownership, allowing
you more time for making money, growing a moustache
or terrorising beasts with the twelve-bore.

*Fig. 2. A factory hand enjoys the increased urgency of production
that only the imminent threat of airborne death can inspire.*

PLAYING
THE GAME

REGRETTABLY, there will be moments in any merchant adventurer's life when the personal qualities of vigour and self-discipline may not alone be sufficient to carry the day. Perhaps Colin, your pygmy valet, has again mistaken gunpowder for ground pepper and you must face down a rogue elephant with a dicky revolver and an even dickier tummy. Or maybe Sir Gilbert, in his exuberance at the gaming table, has staked the factory wages on a hand of penny twist and left you to "straighten it out" with the workers with only a pinch of snuff and the sixpence from last year's Christmas pudding.

In such predicaments, where a man's prospects for success may rest, however briefly, in the hands of others, we must turn to the art of negotiation and the proper application of what I call BIG GAME THEORY.

GAME ON

FROM THE HONEST HAWKER bartering with the heart of a LION to the sly pedlar wheedling with a SERPENT'S cunning, every bargaining position found in commerce has its own mirror in nature. A full and unabridged menagerie of potential negotiating positions and their outcomes is provided overleaf. And while I would always counsel the Tigerish Titan of Industry to stay true to his stripes, he should not be afraid to muddy them in the waterhole where the big cat finds himself in a dogfight. The INNER TIGER who can successfully channel his HUNGRY HIPPO will always outwit the OCELOT.

BITCH SLAP !

INNER TIGER VS. OUTER TIGER
or Zero Sum Game. Tiger wins.

KIAI !

OUTER BOAR VS. CRUSHING BORE
or Zero Rum Game. Bore by a whisker.

GOLDMAN
SACK-BUTT !

INNER MOUSE WITH OUTER RHINO VS. FAT CAT
or Zero Bum Game. Mouse wins, Fat Cat keeps bonus.

ADVANCED (NON-ZERO) SCENARIOS :

OUTER CROC VS. INNER CROOK
Crook cracks, Croc croaks.

OUTER OTTER VS. INNER ROTTER
Score draw.

OUTER DOUBTER VS. INNER DEMONS
Match abandoned.

INNER CITY VS. OUTER RING ROAD
Bypass advised.

INNER GLIMMER VS. WINNER'S DINNERS
Stewards' Inquiry.

Something for the Weekend ?

OFFERED TO THE READER :
TWO DAYS OF VIGOROUS MOTIVATION
AND INSPIRATIONAL INSIGHT

Fully to understand the philosophies and methods of RELEASE THE TIGER, the aspirant alpha male is advised to spend a weekend on one of Sir Roderick "Rocky" Rhodes' Residential Instructional Courses. Held in a 100-acre retreat in fine English countryside, away from the bustle of modern life and the prying eyes of the constabulary, the event is personally hosted by Sir Roderick and includes :

—DAY ONE—

WELCOME LECTURE with coffee, tea, biscuits and roast goose

INSPIRATIONAL ADDRESS with daguerreotypes in Great Hall, including photographic portraits of the host in Africa, riding on top of an elephant, native girl, &c.

PORT

WORKSHOP, where you will be able to observe members of the lower orders toiling in a foundry

SNUFF

LIGHT 17-COURSE SUPPER

SPEECHES

NATIONAL ANTHEM

BED

NOTE : Sir Roderick also offers a Wife Coaching service, where one's spouse can be educated in the practicalities of being The Woman behind the Successful Man.

—DAY TWO—

REVEILLE
NATIONAL ANTHEM
COLD GOOSE
VISIT to nearby Home for the Mentally
Enfeebled (sticks for poking inmates
provided)
PORT
TEAM-BUILDING EXERCISES (fox hunting,
servant bullying, shouting)
SAUTERNES
ROLE-PLAYING SESSION in which we attack
a devotee of Mr Karl Marx with cudgels
CLOSING REMARKS and opportunity to
make donation to the host's charitable
foundation
RELEASE FROM CELLAR of guests who have
made an appropriate donation
CARRIAGES

BEING AN EXAMINATION OF
THE SEVEN AND A HALF HABITS
OF HIGHLY EFFECTIVE VICTORIANS

GIVING A HAND UP TO YOUNG APPRENTICES

IT HAS BEEN ARGUED by several tender-hearted, and soft-headed, commentators that "Youngsters are the future." While we business men of Britain have little time for this sort of namby-pambying towards the next generation, who are often feckless, tearful, small, dirty or all of the above, there is no doubt that youths have their place in commerce. Given his ability to wriggle into small spaces, the cheaper clothing and materials costs involved (rags, chimney sweep brush) and his continuing inability to organise himself into a labour movement, a young apprentice can be an astute acquisition for any business. In exchange for opportunity, investment and training, you may acquire a worker of loyalty whom you can mould in your own image. And in Britain today, nobody is doing better out of the apprentice system than the admirable Lord Spoon of Hackney.

Lord Spoon came from modest beginnings—his father was a mere Baronet—but he vowed not to let his unfortunate start in life hamstring him too severely. By the age of sixteen, he was already jabbing his finger at people and selling them tat from the back of a horse and cart, and it was not long before he had made a fortune via sales of his patented PERSONAL CORRESPONDENCE GENERATOR, RECKONING ABACUS AND FINGER POINTER. These splendid machines aided their owner in quotidian activities such as composing a letter, planning household finances, or having something heavy and durable upon which to take out his frustration when the device suffered one of its periodic bouts of malfunction.

TO RUSSIA WITH LOVE

OF COURSE, the life of the great entrepreneur is never without the occasional upset, and Lord Spoon has known setbacks as well as success. For instance, His Lordship's attempts to annex Russia, claiming a right to the throne by dint of his title the Business Tsar, were broadly catastrophic.

"Your Russian", his Lordship has stated, "is not easily swayed by finger jabbing, no matter how forceful, nor inspirational tales of how one began one's commercial career by selling scrap vegetables out of the back of a pony in the East End. No wonder they are all poor. It is probably the cold weather that makes them rather intransigent, or perhaps their insistence on pretending not to understand bladdy English."

Rebuffed after a bitter failed takeover of Saint Petersburg, Lord Spoon has contented himself instead with the training and mentorship of the young via his Apprentice scheme. The selfless Lord has sought to mentor some of the most intellectually bereft young people in Britain today by offering opportunities in the industries of HOT AIR PRODUCTION and FINANCIAL IRRESPONSIBILITY, and the exciting new science of SELF-DELUSIONAL FOOLISHNESS.

Investment in his Apprentices has provided Lord Spoon with a steady stream of willing workers for his myriad enterprises. Lord Spoon puts them through a gruelling recruitment programme to verify that they have trouble counting to four, are proficient in arguing and can run around shouting meaningless business-babble at the tops of their voices. They are also rigorously vetted to ensure that they can laugh appreciatively at Lord Spoon's famed flights of verbal fancy.

"That is unbelievably important," says his Lordship. "In fact, one might almost say that it is *punbelievably* important," he adds, while his faithful retainer, Hewitt, presents a freshly ironed copy of *The Times* of London with an arched eyebrow.

Sadly, despite the painstaking recruitment process, some of Lord Spoon's young charges have not displayed reciprocal levels of commitment.

"One ran off to become a pirate," says Lord Spoon. "One managed to escape on his first day at work and simply vanished. Several have left my employment to pursue ill-considered careers on the stage. One got herself into trouble. Another one revealed himself to be even more stupid than I had previously thought, fell asleep face down in his bowl of gruel and drowned.

"Overall, though," muses his Lordship, "I usually dismiss them from their posts for my own amusement.

"If I have learned one thing from business, it is that time is bladdy money. Thus one ought never to allow oneself to be detained by anybody for a second longer than one deems necessary," says Lord Spoon, attempting to poke your correspondent in the eye with a sausagey finger. "In conclusion, you are fired. Clear off."

An enlightening interview was then brought to a close with his Lordship setting the dogs, and his beguiling companion Miss Brady, upon your correspondent.

CHAPTER 2

WORKING WITH OTHERS

by Miss Marjorie Penn-Puscher

—

DIRECTOR OF INHUMAN RESOURCES
AT ONE OF THE "BIG FOUR" LIME KILNS

MISS PENN-PUSCHER
BREAKS IN A NEW COLLEAGUE

WITH BRITAIN STRIVING to achieve even greater economic heights, all of us—from the wealthiest factory owner to the lowliest shop girl—are spending longer and longer hours at work. Our cousins on the Continent may slumber through the day, gorging themselves on olives and fornicating under their befuddling hot sun, but we English middle classes and working folk are hard at toil, striving to make our social betters as rich as possible, in the knowledge that their wealth will trickle down to us below as sure as the fierce mother robin regurgitates chewed-up worms into the greedy maws of her darling young chicks.

For is there a nobler calling than that of the Englishman, who rises before dawn to walk the bracing seven miles to his place of work, waving goodbye to his loving wife and seven ruddy, healthy children and giving an especially fond "fare ye well" to his nine sickly ones ? And as he toils there for his allotted four score hours and ten a week (plus Saturdays), does his heart not sing at being part of something, something far greater than he, a tiny cog maybe, but a vital one in the marvellous machine that is England today ?

As we in the Inhuman Resources department are fond of saying : "You do not know how lucky you are to work here." For the modern place of work is not just a locus where a man exchanges his labour for money : it is a social hub, a springboard to opportunity and a moral compass. Let this chapter be your guide as you strive to give of your very best in all facets of your employ. Buzz, buzz, little English bee : our hive needs YOU !

—MARJORIE PENN-PUSCHER

THE PLACE OF WORK :
BLENDING IN
AND STANDING OUT

HOW, THEN, IS ONE TO "FIT IN" at a place of work ?
As in any society, there are rules : sometimes
written, sometimes unwritten and sometimes—in
the more unreconstructed industries of the smoggy
North—tattooed and branded upon the workforce.
Without question, taking up a new employment can be
bewildering in the extreme.

Help is at hand. The splendid new science of
MANAGEMENT (*legal disclaimer—not an actual science*)
takes as one of its central tenets Professor Pluvius
Partington-Partington's "Universal Theory of
Workplace Time and Commotion". In this magnificent,
exhaustive work, Professor Partington-Partington (*legal
disclaimer—not an actual professor*) explains how all
places of work, be they cotton mill, bank, backstreet
apothecary or house of ill repute, conform to the same
basic dynamics.

It is the compelling argument of the Professor that
the person who studies and recognises these dynamics
places himself at an enormous competitive advantage.
First, be aware that an office or factory will have its
HIERARCHY. It should be simple to identify those high up
in the pecking order, the most obvious indicator being
that they are wearing a top hat. However, more subtle
gradations may be difficult to divine : is an individual
being compelled to make tea, laugh at the pleasantries
of another or play golf deliberately inadequately ? He
is most likely a FLUNKY OF NO IMPORTANCE or BITCH.

Top Flight—

Squeezed Middle—

Riff Raff—

Social Climber

FIG. 1. YOUR PLACE OR MINE
The professional hierarchy or PYRAMID.
Pharaohs atop. Wage slaves below.

Success in any organisation is therefore largely a matter of identifying where one stands in the scheme of things, and then dedicating oneself to the twin skills of TOADYING and BULLYING. Do not let intellectual feebleness, incompetence or absence of backbone make you think that you cannot be a man of consequence : dedicate yourself instead to developing the flexibility of body and soul needed for simultaneous bottom-kissing and back-stabbing. Caution should be exercised, as precise identification of the status of the targeted individual is vital : the consequences of a BOTTOM-STABBING can be far-reaching and dreadful for a career.

Away from the cut-and-thrust of playing politics, it is a regrettable fact of modern life that work is largely a struggle against tedium. Indeed, it might be argued that the individual most likely to succeed is often the one with the highest threshold for boredom, and that simply staying awake and conscious longer than one's rivals is the real key to progress, especially in academia, the law and jobs involving the inhalation of a lot of solvents.

Helpful techniques to alleviate boredom and ameliorate your quality of life at work include :

A CIGARETTE BREAK :
> Take a break from smoking for perhaps five minutes every hour.

GATHERING AROUND THE WATER COOLER :
> If you work in a forge or boiler-room, attempt to reduce your body temperature by pressing yourself up against the coolant tanks.

BREAKOUT AREA :
> If you have been sentenced to a few years' hard labour, consider escape.

Having mastered the arts of sycophancy and sneakiness, and proven yourself able to battle manfully against monotony, absorb the Professor's remaining prerequisite for being a valued part of a team in the workplace : DISSEMINATING AMUSING PICTURES OF CATS.

SNOOP MOGGY MOGG

FIG. 2. TYPICAL CAT TAT

Professor Partington-Partington has established that more than 27 per cent of total hours spent at work in Britain today are taken up with photographing, sketching, encaptioning or distributing pictorial representations of felines in adorable or comical pose. There is no surer way to ingratiate oneself in a new job than by joining in with this heart-warming and witless ritual : acquire some pictographic pussycats without delay.

WOMEN AT WORK :
OUGHT THEY
TO BE
ENCOURAGED ?

A FTER MY WELL-RECEIVED recent pamphlet "Children
in the Workplace—The Advantages of Nimble
Little Fingers Against the Menace of Whinging", many
colleagues in the field of Inhuman Resources have asked
for my views on the presence of women at work. I am
in favour—with some important caveats.

First, let me state quite clearly that the so-called
Suffragists are plotting a dangerous course. As I
understand it, these women wish to become involved in
office politics, a preserve as treacherous as it is complex,
and one very much better left to the men. I for one
would find the clever decisions of our brilliant men of
commerce and vigorous financiers far too taxing for my
feminine intellect. I can only gasp in trepidation at the
terrible disarray into which Britain's financial system
might be plunged if men were prevented from deciding
everything unilaterally and without the well-meaning
but silly interference for which our sex is known.

These women would be much better served by
concentrating on exploiting the two major advantages
afforded to ladies by work : something to do in between
having children ; and a place to meet suitable gentlemen.

That the workplace ought to be fertile soil in which
to unearth a husband is self-evident : from the shy
dairy maid who feels herself blushing hotly under
the appraising gaze of a handsome stable boy to the

clever, bookish secretary who finds herself ear-marked for special duties by an attentive older employer, the opportunities for attracting a mate are legion.

FIG. 1. THEIR EYES MET ACROSS A CROWDED LOOM

For this reason, always dress as well as you can afford and take pains with your appearance at work. However, note that there is a world of difference between being the ideal GIRL FRIDAY (demure, fragrant) and getting a reputation as the OFFICE HARLOT (bold, over-perfumed).

FIG. 2.

Respectable Lady of Commerce   *Brazen Hussy*

Besides, the sort of attention that forward behaviour garners is not the sort of attention a lady should want. Remember : no gentleman worth his salt would even consider dipping his pen in the company ink, not least because ink can create the most bothersome stains, and because he might catch something beastly from an improperly maintained inkwell. Be especially vigilant at any Yuletide Festivities if punch or eggnog is being taken, and make it your goal to entice but not excite.

With luck, you ought to attract the very best possible fellow that your physical attributes and social station allow, and you can then get on with woman's right and proper work : having babies and making sure that your husband has a hot meal on the table when he returns from his toil.

ODDS & SODS : LEARNING TO RECOGNISE YOUR COLLEAGUES (AND THEIR QUALITIES)

WHETHER ONE WORKS as a Gin Palace go-between or the Governor of a guano mine, one will invariably encounter the same sorry array of human behaviours. Indeed, my erstwhile patron, Lady Mycroft-Briggs, has proven that every modern worker falls into one of six basic ARCHETYPES or personality disorders.[1] The reader is advised to pay heed to these habitual deviations—shown below—and interact with his colleagues accordingly.

TYPE I.N.T.P.

THE MIXED MESSENGER
Means well and applies himself diligently—
to little effect. Invariably gets the wrong
end of the stick.

---

[1] Mycroft-Briggs, Lady, *A Psychosomatic Typography*, 1863

TYPE R.O.F.L.

THE SHIRKER SHERPA
or MISGUIDED MISSILE

Indolent and insolent in equal measure, the
SHERPA excels in leading others astray.

TYPE O.E.C.D.

TYPE T.T.F.N.

THE ROTTEN EGGHEAD

As sharp as a tack, or
the knife he has just
planted between your
shoulderblades. CLEVER
CLOGS and HEEL.

THE PROBING PROBOSCIS

A YES MAN who never
takes NO for an answer,
the PROBOSCIS has a nose
in every bottom and a
thumb in every pie chart.

TYPE T.N.T.

THE SPUNKY FLUNKY

Lowers the tone while raising the bar. No match for his more able cousin, the INSUBORDINATE SUBORDINATE.

TYPE O.D.B.

THE AUTO CAD

The office bounder, with an instinct for devilry. As liable to make out with the MAID as make off with the STATIONERY.

TYPE R.T.F.M.

THE HEIR HEAD
or INTERMINABLE INTERN

Seconded from Daddy's Estate as part of the WITLESS PROTECTION PROGRAMME.

BUILDING A TEAM

How then is the man of ambition to forge this ragtag assortment of hardy nuts and soft centres into a steely cadre of productive and co-operative workers ? Herewith some suggested excursions that will bind even the most recalcitrant workforce more closely together :

TEAM-BUILDING EXERCISE № 1
WHITE WATER GRAFTING

—

A BEAUTIFUL DAY'S PADDLING UP PSCHITT CREEK IN
WESTPHALIA (PADDLES NOT PROVIDED)

LEVEL : Beginner

ACTIVITY : Descent over rapids while cross-tabulating a novel corporate index card system.

BENEFITS : Unity of purpose. Fish for supper.

№ 2 : CAN WE FIX IT ? YES WE CANYON !

—

BRIDGING THE GAP BETWEEN EXPEKTATION & REALITY, TWIN VILLAGES, CANTON OF CRASS-METAPHØR, NORWAY

LEVEL : Intermediate

ACTIVITY : Constructing a bridge using only two wooden chairs, a piece of string and a small party of native bearers.

BENEFITS : Builds resilience. And a bridge.

№ 3 : MUSICAL CHAIR

—

FULLY IMMERSIVE AURAL ASSAULT COURSE AT THE PRINCE ALBERT SCHOOL OF PERFORMING TARTS, COBHAM

LEVEL : Advanced

ACTIVITY : Listening to the Chairman pluck out his repertoire of Austrian *Nachtwurzelmuzak* on the Company Banjo.

BENEFITS : Survivors will be morally improved.

CHARITY : INCREASINGLY BEGINS AT WORK

ONE OF THE MOST JOYOUS ASPECTS of labouring in a bustling office is the numerous opportunities presented for charitable giving. Sometimes it seems that scarce a day goes past when one is not able to make a donation to a fellow worker's charity pursuits or contribute to a gift for someone.

How splendidly Christian one feels when the trusty brown envelope arrives with a whispered "Eliza has given birth to her fourteenth ; we're having a whip-round", or "Marjorie is doing a sponsored cough to raise money for croup", and one is able to put one's modest wage packet to really selfless, inspiring use by doling it immediately back out to one's colleagues.[1]

Another highly appealing aspect about charity in the workplace is how inventive one can be in finding new ways to raise money. For instance, many gentlemen in recent years have taken to participating in Movember, that most commendable social project where men shave off their moustaches for the entirety of a month. God bless those cheerful cards with their upper-lip tomfoolery !

We should be in awe of our fellow workers who undertake such projects, which they do out of self-effacing concern for poorly puppies or starving infants in the Namib desert or whatsoever it might be, and not in any way to draw attention to themselves and lord it over others with their moral superiority.

---

[1] Note : We are hearing upsetting reports of the concept of the "whip-round" being taken literally. The flogging of employees until they contribute to the cost of repairs to the factory chapel roof simply will not do.

BEING AN EXAMINATION OF
THE SEVEN AND A HALF HABITS
OF HIGHLY EFFECTIVE VICTORIANS

LISTENING CAREFULLY
TO SUBORDINATES
AND THEN IGNORING
THEM COMPLETELY

W E HAVE DISCUSSED in this chapter the legion challenges and occasional joys of working alongside one's fellow man. Each of us, from the plainest mill weevil to the most important financier, is a leaf on the tree of British commerce, doing our part to help the trunk grow ever thicker, sturdier and more imposingly towering above all those silly little foreign bushes in the world's great forest. However, the fact remains that small leaves must die and fall off, turn to mulch and thus help the really big and significant leaves to become even more fine and splendid.

Men of accomplishment know well that the common herd too often have their own ideas about how business ought to be done, and while these ideas can conceivably be of passing interest, they must never be allowed to distract the entrepreneurial visionary from his purpose. And no one typifies this belief more than the celebrated American inventor Mr Jedediah Applebore-Jobbs.

Mr Applebore-Jobbs, who has swept all before him with his magnificent range of portable musical boxes, slate tablets upon which amusing parlour games may be sketched out and sundry other time-wasting devices, is a man who knows his own mind.

"And let me tell you another thing," interrupts Mr Applebore-Jobbs. "In a few years I will be able to know everybody else's mind as well."

It is true : the great inventor is developing a top hat that will perform musical compositions of the wearer's choice, provide storage for family portraits, tell him where he is on a map and furnish him with sundry other devilments with which to amuse his friends and bamboozle his enemies. It may even be that the hats will have practical capabilities for commerce or creation.

It is the dream of Mr Applebore-Jobbs that one day every coffee house in the land will be filled with people sporting his millinery and pretending to write novels. What is more, he hopes that the hats will eventually be able to see inside a man's most private thoughts.

"Quite often, one of my workers will say, 'But sir, how can we possibly manufacture a hat that can know the inside of man's heart and mind, for surely that is the preserve of God alone ?' and I will say, 'I know— that is why I can do it.'

"I have frequently had to dismiss an employee for refusing to believe I am a supernatural being," says Mr Applebore-Jobbs. "That, and for building top hats that weigh the same as one of Mr Kingdom Brunel's bridges."

NO IFS OR BUTTONS

IT IS THE CONTENTION of Mr Applebore-Jobbs that in the future, humans will be replaced by shiny white automatons who might be controlled by a single button, and he works all hours to ensure this becomes a reality.

"Never let your course be diverted by an underling who refuses to believe you can alter the laws of physics, reason or motion," cautions the great inventor. "For to be in charge is to be right and, in time, the world will be ready for a musical, mind-reading hat the size of the Clifton Suspension Bridge.

"And I shall make my detractors and naysayers eat it," he says. "I wonder how they will like those apples ?"

A valuable lesson, then : listen to all, and then do exactly as you please.

Introducing

MICRO-TOFF OFFICE 1895

WRITES

READS

ADDS UP

POINTS

POSTS

SIPS TEA

The Better Class of Clerk

Guaranteed to be free from all Bed Bugs, Common Viruses & Worms

FULLY COMPATIBLE WITH
**MICRO-TOFF OFFICE
FOR WIDOWS***

**FREE MEMORY STICK
WITH EVERY ORDER**
"Beat them until they remember"

Install a Micro-Toff in your Chambers today
and receive a complimentary Micro-Toff Wordsmith,
Micro-Toff Look-Out & Micro-Toff Look-Out Expressly.

*May not be true

Chapter 3

LEADING FROM BEHIND THE FRONT

by Colonel Tobermory 'Mojo' Scarper

8th royal prancers

A Chip off the old Blockhead.
Mojo spends some quality time
with his son, Mojito

THIRTY-FIVE YEARS OF SERVICE in the British Army taught me a great many things, and I believe that much of what I have learned—with the possible exception of how to bayonet a rival—may be very well applied to modern commerce.

In war, as in times of economic uncertainty, unthinking respect for authority is paramount and must be enforced at all costs. While fighting for Queen, Country and the life-affirming sound of leather on firm young flesh, I saw many bloodthirsty foreigners at uncomfortably close quarters. Villainous Mahdists, rampaging Afghans and the snivelling pacifists of the Red Cross are all beastly sights, but none was more hair-raising than that of the wrath of Major General Kitchener when a young *aide-de-camp* baulked at Kitchener's request to pop into his tent and check if he had something in his moustaches.

On quiet nights, I fancy I can still hear the cries of that young officer as Kitchener set him straight about the chain of command (and the basics of moustache maintenance). Unfortunately, the do-gooders have had their way and similar disciplinary techniques are now outlawed in the modern workplace, but the principle of "Thrash first and ask questions later" is never a bad one in dealing with underlings. In the mess, in the boardroom and in the bedroom, discipline is all.

Likewise, the officer's maxim "Never ask of your men what you would not do yourself" has much to commend it when applied to both soldiering and industry, by illustrating the enormous amount of rhubarb that is talked today. The whole point of having flunkies is to make them perform all the demeaning and tedious functions which are beneath one's own station, and in this chapter I shall demonstrate exactly how to lick your own rabble into shape.

—MOJO

LEADERSHIP : IT'S TOFF AT THE TOP

IN THE GLORIOUS and bloody days of yore, a general would charge at the head of his army as did Alexander of Macedon when he routed Darius at Issus, or my grandfather Cairngorm Botchitt-Scarper—known to all as "Terry"—when he stuck it to an entire hamlet of Zanzibari tribeswomen with nothing but four regiments and a small Navy for support.

By regrettable contrast, we old soldiers of rank in the modern British Army must stay some miles behind the front line, planning, inspiring, leading and ensuring that the chaps have somebody to look up to. For what would be the sense in the world being deprived of my near four decades of military experience by a sudden stray spear or wildly swung native axe ? None whatsoever.

As I sit in my tent with the other greybeards, a batman or two trying to keep my spirits up with a glass of something, a punkawallah punkawallah-ing away, I often think how much I should love to be getting shot at with the young bucks. Sadly those days are now behind me. But I take some comfort in the fact that I can pass on my expertise to other officers, and succour in the knowledge that my service for Queen and Country might also be a source of inspiration for captains of industry.

Broadly speaking, a large factory or firm runs along the same lines as a regiment. At the bottom, you have unskilled labour, analogous to the Army's Other Ranks, who do the heavy-lifting in often dangerous conditions and should be shot for desertion wherever possible *pour encourager les autres*. A class of experienced enlisted men, chosen for their short stature and love of shouting, act as Foremen or NCOs ; while day-to-day operations are overseen by the Junior Officers or Middle Managers. Atop the pyramid, ideally in a very comfortable chair, sits the Regimental Colonel or Grand Poobah, i.e. me and, if you are any sort of fellow at all, you.

The 3rd Ottoman Campaign

Thanks to the meddling of our Leftist friends, the days when one could ensure discipline in a workplace by shooting a bad apple have passed ; and the top man of today must learn how to lead without recourse to capital punishment. As I embarked on my second career in the mining business, I found considerable useful instruction in an excellent tome entitled THE ONE MINUTE MANAGER. As I recall, this neat little book contends that a chap can get all his motivational and leadership duties out of the way in one minute each day. I would gather the workers around, climb on top of a chair and shout at them all at once ; this provided a useful economy of scale and allowed me to spend the rest of the day on more pressing matters. In especially busy times, I adopted the position of THE ONE SECOND MANAGER, where I would have my staff line up and then gallop past them on my horse bellowing at breakneck speed. Morale, it is fair to say, soared.

Occasionally, it may be necessary to speak one-on-one with a subordinate. This is perhaps the most delicate and difficult facet of leadership, but I am happy to pass on a little technique I call THE CARROT AND THE STICK. The reader would be quite amazed how quickly a lackey can be made to see one's point of view if one hits him hard enough and often enough with a decent-sized carrot.[1]

Just as the enlisted man is sometimes slow to see the glory of charging forward into a well-armed, numerically superior enemy, so can the worker be ungrateful for the marvellous opportunities afforded him to improve his  physique and burnish his strength of character by tough and demanding labour. One might think that he would simply be grateful for the employment, and the chance to contribute to Britain's ongoing success. Sadly the modern solider, like the modern drudge, requires coddling rather than the cosh. It is your mission, commander, to inspire him.

---

[1] Other root vegetables also available.

WHICH TYPE OF LEADER ARE YOU ?

THE STUDENT OF MANAGEMENT draws inspiration from history's great leaders. Be it the wisdom of Solomon, the sweeping ambition of Charlemagne or the immaculate chin beard of Philip II, there are sundry exemplars in the pages of mankind's achievements. Identify a historical leader whose style best fits your own and tailor your strategies accordingly.

TYPE A—Are you instinctive and quick-thinking, relying often on flashes of inspiration in your business decisions that may seem capricious to outsiders ? It may be that you are a CALIGULA. Do not attempt to appoint a favoured horse to high rank in your organisation, and try to steer clear of female relatives in the workplace.

Fig. 1. Whinney the Poobah.

TYPE B—Are you constantly looking to expand the horizons of your enterprise, forcing your way into new markets by fair means or foul, and wishing to crush competitors, especially foreigners ? If not, you surely ought to be ; if so, perhaps you take your inspiration from GENGHIS KHAN. Let nothing limit your ambition, for the empire that does not expand will soon collapse in on itself. It is probably no longer necessary to ride around on horseback with a spear, however, and having a harem of 2,000 courtesans is not to be encouraged owing to considerations of space, if nothing else.

TYPE C—If you are sometimes quite harsh with your subordinates and find yourself wanting to make an example of unsatisfactory workers, you may be a VLAD THE IMPALER. Note well, though, that a boss who favours sticking employees on a wooden spike may find that he gets a splinter or two himself in the process from time to time.

Fig. 2. Mr Impaler engages with a stakeholder.

TYPE D—Sitting around for long periods of time and looking at spiders suggests you may be a ROBERT THE BRUCE, or possibly a MISS MUFFET. Beware conflicts with your neighbours, and avoid outdoor picnics.

TYPE E—If you have a terrier-like personality, boundless ambition and a sense of inferiority for which you constantly overcompensate, you may be a NAPOLEON. If you are short in stature, do not conduct business with your hand halfway inside your waistcoat, and be cautious of taking a wife who has a highly strung or amorous temperament. Avoid business ventures in Corsica.

Fig. 3.
Boney : Show
Pony.

TYPE F—Any readers of the gentler sex might well look at the case of JOAN OF ARC. Of course, in the modern era, nobody would suggest that an ambitious and successful female ought to be burned at the stake as a witch. Nonetheless, ladies, a cautionary tale is a cautionary tale.

WHO MOVED MY STILTON ?

LESSONS FROM ANTIQUITY

M Y OWN STYLE OF LEADERSHIP is often compared
to that of Nero, erstwhile Roman Emperor
and coffee-house entrepreneur. But while I share his
ardour for overpriced almond pastries and matricidal
Mediterranean cruises, I draw my own inspiration from
a far greater figure from the ancient world ...

HERCULES !
Beacon of muscular project management ; Hero of
indefatigable corporate resourcefulness.

HERCULES !
Self-starting multi-tasker with a hotline to
upper management.

HERCULES !
Saviour of Prometheus ; Slayer of Poseidon ; Leading
Consultant to the sporting fashion industry.

And all this from a young man sporting a toga and
open-toed sandals. Imagine what he might have achieved
with a pair of steel-capped jackboots and a fistful of
British sabre !
The tale of Hercules remains the perfect guide to
a life in business. It is no accident that his twelve
tasks should mirror *precisely* the twelve steps the
skilful capitalist must take to cement his position atop
the greasy pole. Hence I have made Mr Poppinjay's
notoriously vivid *Bumper Book of Myths* required
reading for all my adjutants.

THE 12 STEPS TO HERCULEAN SUCCESS

TASK 1   TAMING THE NEMEAN LINE MANAGER
Be swift in showing your subordinates who is boss. Do not tolerate open displays of dissent or the wearing of expensive fur coats.

TASK 2   SLAYING THE NINE-HEADED HYDRA
Address issues of headcount early and decisively. Be bold when cutting over-heads or tackling inefficiency and waste.

TASK 3   CAPTURING THE GOLDEN BEHIND OF ARTEMIS
Speed is all. Identify the most esteemed behinds to kiss and pucker up accordingly.

TASK 4   CAPTURING THE ERYMANTHIAN BOARDROOM
Choose your allies carefully. Favour those who can hold their drink.

TASK 5   CLEANING THE AUGEAN STABLES
Tolerate no ordure from your underlings. Even the most insurmountable task may be made possible through the diversion of resources.

TASK 6   KILLING THE STYMPHALIAN BIRDS
Take great care when dealing with man-eating vultures, or bankers.

TASK 7   TAMING THE CRETAN CASH COW
Decide which parts of your business may be exploited for the greatest profit at minimal risk to capital and milk them remorselessly.

TASK 8   RUSTLING THE MARES OF DIOMEDES
Consider starting a company cart scheme for loyal employees. Reserved parking spaces will help avoid unnecessary arguments and/or fire-breathing horses setting each other alight.

TASK 9   PURLOINING THE GIRDLE OF HIPPOLYTA, QUEEN OF THE AMAZONS
Set aside some time each day for relaxation or a little light cross-dressing.

TASK 10 HERDING THE CATTLE OF THE THREE-HEADED MONSTER GERYON
If you practise diversity in the workplace make sure you allocate adequate resources to deal with disability issues.

TASK 11 SCRUMPING THE GOLDEN APPLE OF HESPERIDES
Encourage all your workers to pay into their company pensions. Look after this money carefully—you may need it one day to pay for home renovations or a daughter's wedding.

TASK 12 FETCHING CERBERUS FROM THE GATES OF HELL
Always employ the most fearsome receptionist-gatekeeper money will buy.

HOW TO TALK TO THE LITTLE PEOPLE

THE SUCCESSFUL INDUSTRIALIST faces many challenges, but none more daunting than that of interacting with the lower orders in a conversational setting. What on earth is one to say to the Johnny polishing one's shoes? Or the cleaner woman who inadvertently stumbles in while one is enjoying a well-earned nap late of an afternoon ? Or even, horror of horrors, the funny little operator man if one becomes trapped in his automatic vertical elevation apparatus ?

The illusion that one is interested in the common herd can be most useful in commerce, garnering one a reputation as a versatile thinker, a man of the people and a fellow who can always spot an opportunity.

Have a few prepared phrases and topics of conversation up your sleeve, and you ought to be able to pass a minute or two in relative comfort. The working classes tend to be interested in :

ASSOCIATION FOOTBALL
>Disappointing performance of local teams ; conniving ways of foreign players

MUSIC HALL COMPETITIONS
>Notably Mister Solomon Cowell's ubiquitous "talent" contest, *The XVII Factorum*

THE ONGOING STRICTLY BALLROOM EXTRAVAGANZA
>Especially the health and longevity of its veteran ringmaster, Mister Forsyth-Saga

ILLNESSES
>suffered by themselves or their family members

GIN

SPECULATION
>as to the sort of dresses the Royal Princesses are wearing this season

TRAFFIC CONGESTION

Stick to these topics—and these alone—and you ought to be on sure ground. Never attempt to discuss money or politics with the lower orders, for obvious reasons, and beware that they can become extremely agitated about the myriad failings of the national football XI.

BEING AN EXAMINATION OF
THE SEVEN AND A HALF HABITS
OF HIGHLY EFFECTIVE VICTORIANS

No 3

EATING UP EVERYTHING THAT IS PUT IN FRONT OF YOU (AND EVERYONE ELSE)

THE LITERATURE OF SELF-IMPROVEMENT for industrialists and men of business is as broad as it is deep. But ask yourself this, dear reader : what, other than the usefulness of clever mnemonics and acronyms, do all of these books stress without exception ?

The answer ?

The paramount importance of appetite.

The difference between the man of modest achievement and the powerful man is often no more than a matter of hunger. In animal societies, the creature who desires the most, and takes the most, grows stronger and more powerful than his rivals, allowing him to live in the most luxuriant den, sett, eyrie, sty, &c. and copulate enthusiastically with his pick of the lady creatures. And as in the animal kingdom, so in the world of finance.

One gentleman who has been an inspiration to many is the brilliant Scots financier Mr "Fat" Freddie Foodbinne, who rose from quite humble origins to be one of the most celebrated merchant bankers of our times. He has been kind enough to share a few crumbs from his table for our little book.

"Mother and Father did not have a great deal of money, and I had fourteen brothers and sisters," recalls Mr Foodbinne. "At mealtimes, we had just a pot of gruel and a bowl of tattie-wee between the seventeen of us, and it was a powerful hard struggle to get your share.

"My initial technique was simply to snatch as many of the plates as I could and shovel the food into my mouth before my parents intervened. While this was effective, there was only so much I could grab hold of at once, so I soon formulated a more cunning method.

"I told my sweet, trusting younger siblings that if they gave me some of their gruel today, I would pay them back in delicious treats later. After they taught us Mr Dickens's *Christmas Carol* in school, my wee sister Agnes became determined one day to taste roast turkey for herself. Imagine a wee lassie from Glasgow with such an unrealistic ambition : there could be no way she would ever possibly be able to afford turkey, and such an aspiration would surely drive her into penury, debt, misery and the poorhouse. I spotted an opportunity right away.

IT'S GRUEL TO BE KIND

"I PROMISED HER if she gave me all of her gruel for a year, and her spare pennies from her job in the asbestos pillow factory, I would give her the money for a muckle big turkey of her own at Yuletide. Mother and father were unsure about this at first, but I told them it was important that they create an environment in which enterprise could flourish, or else I should go and live in Aberdeen or some such place.

"Of course, when Christmas came around, I simply explained to Agnes that due to circumstances beyond my control and the fluctuations of the gruel market, there was no money for her turkey," says Mr Foodbinne with a laugh. "She was taken terrible ill with malnutrition, so mother and father had to give her their own bowls of gruel for weeks on end. They asked me for some of the pennies with which to buy more food for the family, but fortunately I had hidden them away safely and they could not get at them.

"That turkey was delicious," confirms Mr Foodbinne. "And it taught me a very valuable lesson : there are two sorts of people in life. Thin ones, and fat ones, and it is much more desirable to be in the latter category."

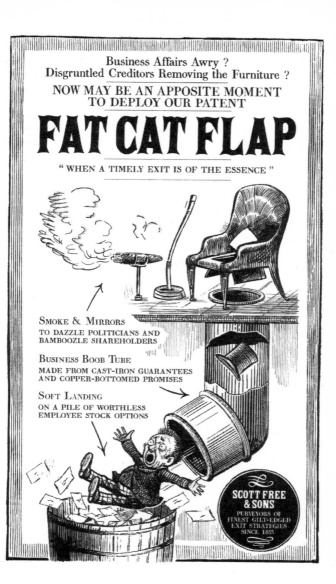

CHAPTER 4

THE ARTS OF PERSUASION

BY RUFUS RATCHETT

—

SHOWMAN & PROFESSIONAL NORTHERNER

Mr Ratchett's prize sow, Notorious P.I.G.

FIRST
PRIZE
PIGS WITH
WIGS
1879

GOLD
MEDAL
FINE SWINE
SOCIETY
1880

PINK
ROSETTE
PORKS FOR
FORKS
1881

PEOPLE ASK WHERE IT ALL BEGAN FOR ME. I tell them : pigs. As a lad in Rochdale, I lived in a ditch outside the back of the workhouse, nose pressed up against the window, watching them lucky orphans inside gorging themselves on gruel and regular beatings. I thought : "I want a bit of that."

The workhouse held competitions to win an apprenticeship in local trades. I entered "Rochdale's Got Butchers" in 1859 and won. It changed my life. By the time I was five I could gut a pig. By seven, I was doing it with my teeth to save money on knives.

I worked my way up. By nine I had my first shop. By eleven, they talked of my pork scratchings from Bury to Oldham. At twelve, I had what I now understand to be a mid-life crisis. I was the Alexander the Great of North-west butchery : there were no worlds left to conquer, and I wept salt tears. Pork had lost its lustre.

I wandered the North, lost. I found myself on Wigan Pier, where I met a travelling entertainer with a monkey and a barrel organ. His act was awful, pathetic. Monkey were the talented one. But people were queuing to watch, giving him pennies a time. I asked him how he did it ; he said it was all down to "advertising". He had a sign claiming the monkey were a second cousin of Queen Victoria, and that listening to the organ music could cure typhoid.

It was like a light went on. I turned away from economy-grade meat and devoted my life to these new arts of salesmanship, marketeering and advertisational dishonesty. Here, I will explain how I did it—and how you too can master the arts of persuasion. And without having to kill pigs, neither.

RR

A HUNGER
TO MONGER

PRECIOUS MINERALS. Lethal home-made alcohol. Primitive bead-based currencies. Spears. Wild monkeys. What do all of these goods have in common ? Other than that they are all available in the mysterious continent of Africa, and in fact the less salubrious parts of my home town of Rochdale, all of them, like any other property, have to be sold to a customer by means of SALES TECHNIQUES.

No matter how revolutionary or remarkable a product, the customer needs to be convinced to a greater or lesser degree. Even my greatest innovation—the Pot Luck Sausage, a delicious tube of fleshy goodness which came with a free draught of indigestion tonic for any customer who could guess the animal or entity from whence it came—faced considerable initial resistance.

It is the task of the manufacturer to persuade the public that they simply cannot carry on living without the product in question. On a local level, it may be possible for the tradesman to impress upon a physically weaker customer that he simply *will not* carry on living unless he purchases a reasonable amount of the product on offer, but violent coercion is a very hard sales technique to employ in the global marketplace, unless one has a substantial military capability.

For example, Her Majesty's Navy has done excellent work in the technique of GUNBOAT DIPLOMACY, and its economic cousin GUNBOAT MARKETING, by convincing the Chinese of the desirability of opium, but this sort of operation is likely out of the reach of most small or medium-sized enterprises.

That being said, there are few products whose desirability to the customer cannot be increased by the addition of opium or other derivatives of the poppy. My biggest-selling product for many years was Ratchett's Smacky Banger, a toothsome sausage comprising of sixty-six per cent rusk, thirty per cent brick dust, three per cent pork-type meat and a pinch of the finest opium. My customers were queuing out of the door for a hundred yards or more, shivering and pleading for another half-a-dozen links, and if you cannot take that to the bank, sir, then I am a Dutchman.

FIG. 1. MORE SATISFIED CUSTOMERS

Even if you cannot literally insert addictive substances into your product, you can do so figuratively by convincing people that your goods are indispensable. It is important to understand that you are not selling a sausage : you are selling a dream, a better life, an escape from the hideous privations of living in Rochdale. Do not simply tell your customers what the product is ; inform them of the benefits accruing to them if they should purchase it : health, wealth, happiness, a chance to become intimately acquainted with attractive members of the opposite sex.

Englishmen of stations both high and low tend to want the same things from life : sporting entertainment, more than enough to drink, a wife who does not talk too much, amusing wordplay about bodily functions and a decent distance between themselves and foreigners. Let your products promise these, and wealth will follow.

Speaking of foreigners, if you are selling your products abroad, ask yourself what it is that the foreign customer wants. Is it the firm reassuring leadership of a man from the civilised world ? A railway ? Some species of shiny button ? Each customer is a lock who can be unpicked with the right key, and that key is the words with which you describe the product. In the next few pages, we shall examine the dark arts of MARKETEERING and ADVERTISEMENTALISING ; for the time being, let me stress quite clearly : "Sell the sizzle, not the sausage—especially when the sausage itself is made of potentially fatal ingredients."

SPEAK SOFTLY AND CARRY A BIG SCHTICK

IN THE EARLIEST YEARS OF COMMERCE, the acquiring of customers were a simple business, usually conducted under cover of darkness and involving the repeated application of a large cudgel.

However, as the number of traders in any given market grew, it became important for a man to distinguish himself from his rivals. By the time of the Norman Conquest, robber barons such as Sieur d'Ogilvy were painting their customer-gathering weaponry in different colours, and employing craftsmen to manufacture eye-catching wooden sticks to wave in village marketplaces. The practice of MARKETEERING[1] was born.

Brandishing his stick, or "log", the earliest marketeer would appraise his clients of an imminent assault with a cheery battle cry : "Log Ho !"

And while the modern salesman is no longer at liberty to flourish his log in public, the tradition of brandishing a "Log Ho !" or BRAND'ING A LOG'O[2] as it has become known, has persisted.

FIG. 1. AN EARLY LOG'O STICK

---

[1] Not to be confused with *Meerkateering*, which is the beating of customers with stuffed novelty toys.
[2] For more on this subject, see the excellent *No Log Ho* by Naomi Kleinenachtmuzik, Kartoffelkopf Press, 1889.

NO PAIN, NO GAIN

Whether beating customers around the head with
coloured logs, searing a ranchers' mark into the
haunches of a Hereford Dipstick or devising a new
corporate monogram, the process of branding remains a
thoroughly painful one, usually undertaken by cowboys.
Upon receipt of a large pile of banknotes, these clever
men can transform your pedestrian company name into
a muddling motif of esoteric appeal.

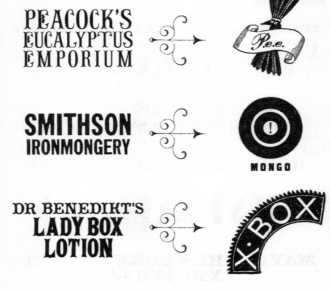

FIG. 2. THE MAGIC OF BRANDING AT WORK

SLOGANEERING†

WITH YOUR BAFFLING INSIGNIA now proudly affixed to every corporate orifice, the next requirement is a SLOGAN—a brief, yet memorable arrangement of words composed by a professional charlatan or word-weaseller.

The ideal SLOGAN should seek to convey your product's noblest ambitions while at the same time upholstering the truth with an array of seductive adjectives to delude the weak of mind and befuddle the unwary. In the likely event that an original slogan is outwith the wit of your weaseller, it is quite acceptable to appropriate someone else's :

THE CART IN FRONT IS A STRAW BOATER

EVERY LITTLE WHELPS

REFRESHES THE PARTS
OTHER PEERS CANNOT REACH

IT DOES EXACTLY WHAT IT SAYS ON THE TIN MINER

JUST DUEL IT !

MAYBE SHE'S BORN WITH IT ;
MAYBE IT'S GOUT

---

† Not to be confused with *Buccaneering*, which generally takes place at sea and with fewer pirates.

MARKETEERING

YOUR LOG'O AND SLOGAN THUS DEVISED, the final step is to place them before the customer, using one of the following tried and tested means :

I. DIRECT MARKETEERING

II. SLIGHTLY MORE DIRECT MARKETEERING

III. Extremely Direct Marketeering

IV. Gorilla Marketeering‡

---

‡ Also known as *Sandwich Boarding*, after the Earl of Sandwich, who pioneered the art of parading tawdry sales messages in public. Not to be confused with *Smorgasboarding*, the parading of open sandwiches in public.

THAT'S ENTERTAINMENT !

BE IT A PIE AND A PINT for the biggest pork buyers in Rochdale or a champagne evening at the Ritz for the big nibs of London industry, the deployment of UNGENTLEMANLY HOSPITALITY FOR GENTLEMEN is the oil that makes the engine of commerce run smooth. Studies of a somewhat scientific nature by the University of Wigan Pier have shown that firms who entertain their important customers in the lavish manner claim higher profits, or at the very least higher spirits.

By the by, research also suggests that employees who have been carefully and remorselessly exploited each year can yet be hoodwinked by a few pennies spent on a YULETIDE SHINDIG into believing that the management considers them valuable cogs in the machine. In short, there is little in business that cannot be boosted by the application of a few bottles of the right stuff.

Many large firms have recognised that important deals can be struck in a more salubrious and lubricated manner away from the place of work. Not only do these "jollies" offer excellent opportunities for business to be done, but they also afford the host firm's representatives an ideal excuse for staying out until all hours behaving in a reprehensible manner.

What wife can successfully gainsay the argument : "Drunk I may be, darling, but I was under compulsion in the service of the firm and only did it to provide for you and our little ones ; now please may I come in because it is fearsome cold on this doorstep and I seem to have lost my pantaloons in an audience-participation burlesque performance ?"

Better to grease those wheels, consider inviting associates to amusing diversions such as a display at a

ALL THE FUN OF THE FAIR MAIDEN

"fully ankle-revealing" gentleman's private club, where women of unquestionable lack of virtue show off their lower legs for money.

Be aware that wealthy customers in any industry will be courted by your rivals also, and recognise that you may need to "top" their efforts in order to impress. If your competitor invites an investor to an evening at the opera, go one better : arrange a private box at the local house of ill-repute. If he suggests an evening of Sauternes-tasting in an fashionable private club, do the same—and then take the party onwards to a backstreet establishment where glasses of laudanum are served and unlicensed sword play is encouraged.

If he should suggest a day of the modish "black-balling"—where men of influence dash around the greensward shooting shotgun cartridges of paint at one another and voting to disbar the inaccurate from their clubs—go yet further and replace the dye ammunition with buckshot. Of course, in this instance, you will need a healthy supply of unarmed workers for your dignitaries to pepper ; but they will surely enjoy the chance to join in the fun with the great and the good.

If a banquet looms, consider engaging the greatest musical talents of the day to perform privately. A short recital from Lord and Lady Ga-Ga could be the absolute talk of the season in the City ; and one firm last winter achieved a splendidly festive event by treating valued investors to a behind-closed-doors sermon from none other than the popular tubthumper Billy "Two Hells" Brimstone.

The wealthy man, like any other, likes to enjoy himself where possible, and it is an undeniable fact that large quantities of alcohol, flattery and sanctioned bad behaviour never tightened any purse-strings. As William Gladstone himself said : "You have to speculate to accumulate—especially in a striptease parlour."

A WORD ON ROYALTY

THE ORIGIN OF THE MAXIM that "The Customer is King" is disputed. Some claim it were first coined by Saint Theo, the mythical Dragon Lord of Cyprus ; some Medieval historians identify it as the family crest of the Baron Philippe de la Greene, the first feudal lord to sell clothing to the peasantry. Regardless of the phrase's origin, there is much wisdom within.

The customer is king indeed. What is more, with the multitudinous royal families of Europe being so keen on breeding, and the increased opportunities for foreign travel afforded to the wealthy by the so-called "Bucket Flights" of the wily Greek Mr Stavros Lutonparkwayos and his fleet of EasyBalloons, the chance of meeting and doing business with an *actual* King is now significant.

Securing a relationship with a royal customer can be the making of any business. Queen Victoria's imprimatur "By Royal Appointment" has been of great commercial value to manufacturers of biscuits, conserves, giant hats, swan defence-mechanisms and Prince Alberts, to name but a few. How I would love to get Her Majesty's face on my Ratchett's Six-Inch Banger.

However, dealing with a royal customer can be tough. Never look them direct in the eye : not only is this disrespectful, but there is a chance they may be descended from a basilisk. Never haggle with anyone of the rank of Marquis or higher ; proposing a "Buy One Get One Free" offer to a member of the royal family is treason.

Finally, beware a dangerous confidence trickster who claims to be the Duchess of York and attempts to hoodwink industrialists into parting with money in exchange for introductions to her husband. She is quite deranged, and may attempt to feast on your feet.

BEING AN EXAMINATION OF
THE SEVEN AND A HALF HABITS
OF HIGHLY EFFECTIVE VICTORIANS

Nº 4

BEING AT ALL TIMES SERIOUS ; AND NEVER GAMBLING UPON THE CRAP-SHOOT THAT IS THE BANDYING OF PLEASANTRIES IN PUBLIC

THERE IS A GROWING TENDENCY in the discussion of business and manufacturing for self-appointed experts to declare that "The Customer is always right." This sort of rot, like much of the nonsense that pollutes our age, is imported from our vigorous, well-meaning, yet empty-headed cousins in the United States of America. In point of fact, the customer is often of feeble intellect, lacking in good taste or judgement, or simply rather common.

The businessman of wisdom and vision, however, does not allow the customer to understand this. He beguiles, he flatters, he offers two-for-one discounts on high days and holidays. It is said of the Englishman that he is the only nationality of fellow who would nick a ball behind to the wicket-keeper and walk before the umpire's finger goes up, but unlike in cricket, it is sadly the case that the game of business is not an arena where honesty is the best policy.

The next gentleman in our instructive series is offered as an example that one man's moral courage can be another man's commercial undoing. Yet it is the world, not he, who ought to be having a long hard look in the mirror. He can hold his head high, square his shoulders and shoot his sleeves to reveal an exquisitely designed pair of six-carat brass cufflinks that will stand the test of time although sadly not water or salty sea air (no refunds available).

RAT-A-TAT TAT

IN A RECENT SPEECH to the Worshipful Foundation of Directorial Grand High Wizards at the Royal Albert Hall, the powerful jewellery manufacturer Mr Gerrard Ratfink amused his audience by outlining in precise detail the sort of person who might purchase his products.

"We manufacture a silver salver for sherry glasses of somewhat gaudy design," Mr Ratfink confessed to an enthralled company. "I suspect that some of the butlers who might serve from it would be of not quite the highest rank," he said, to nervous laughter from the audience.

"I did even hear of a woman in Harrogate who purchased one of these trays and allowed her scullery maid to polish it rather than her senior housemaid !" continued Mr Ratfink to shocked gasps from the assembled gentlemen.

Mr Ratfink apologised for any embarrassment he

might have caused and stressed that he had, of course, been speaking humorously.

However, the damage was done.

Within weeks, ever more lurid tales began to appear in the penny press of Ratfink's silverware being used to present inferior Madeira to guests, being roughly scrubbed by an underfootman and, in one instance, of a Wiltshire lady who wished to remain anonymous being offered a glass of red wine on one—*to accompany her fish course.*

Ratfink was ruined. A family business that had once provided a satisfactory income for dozens of cousins and Ratfink relatives saw its value on the stock market obliterated almost overnight. Ratfink himself was reduced to selling prawn sandwiches from a stall on Cheapside ; the situation grew so bad that he could not even afford the fishy ingredients and had to barter his patented silver-effect ear-rings to acquire the shellfish. Let his experience be a warning to any would-be retailer : never tell the truth, and certainly not in public.

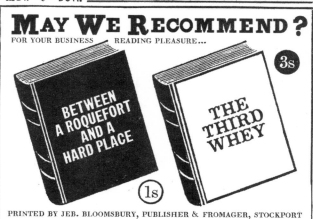

THE SCIENCE OF COMMERCE

BY JEAN-PIERRE CAMEMBERT

PROFESSOR OF WORKING LUNCHEON STUDIES
UNIVERSITY OF PARIS IX

PROFESSOR CAMEMBERT SETS IN MOTION
HIS LASTEST SCIENTIFIC MARVEL,
THE LARGE CABRON COLLIDER

WE IN FRANCE FIND MUCH TO ADMIRE IN BRITAIN : the generous proportions of your womenfolk's figures, your quaint ideas of waiting one behind the other in your famous "queues", your enthusiasm for the "bing drinking" and the having of the punch-ups abroad which has made the British Empire rightly feared across the globe.

In industry you have also shown the rest of the world the way, and while we on the Continent were busy growing our tomato plants, making delicious sauces with butter or chopping each other's heads off, you English set about getting rich and powerful with your mining, shipbuilding and manufacturing of the amusing Toby's Jugs with their ugly little faces. Bravo, English chums !

But the world is changing also. Americans, Orientals and Teutonic peoples will be catching up fast, and Britain must act decisively to keep from being left on a sticky wickets, as you say in your famously unwatchable summer pastime. In this chapter, I humbly present some of my findings on how science and technology are coming to bear upon industry, and urge all my British friends to consider them. Perhaps one day our two great nations can work in harmony to achieve a Continental harmony and shared financial greatness, or at the least to avoid being bossed around by *Les Allemands*.

I hope you enjoy my little dish and wish you *bon appétit* !

—J.-P.C.

"A BIRD IN THE PAN IS WORTH TWO IN THE BURNING BUSH"

—TRADITIONAL PROVENÇAL SAYING

FOR TWELVE LONG YEARS at the Centre for Working Luncheon Studies, we pondered and experimented upon our UNIFIED THEORY OF MODERN COMMERCE. I confess that at times the project seemed too large, too monstrous, too *ridicule*, like an American waddling around the Louvre in search of the *Mona Lisa*.

Or so I felt, until we had a wonderful moment of breaking-through last year.

It was a Tuesday in April. We had laboured without rest for several minutes in the morning and, *naturellement*, we were ready for lunch. We broke for a light meal of *ortolan*. I do not believe this delicious dish is very common in England so I shall describe briefly. It is a small songbird, captured and blinded and then overfed in a cage, before being drowned in brandy and roasted. Some like to burn down the bird's nest as well and urinate upon the smouldering remains, but that is increasingly considered vindictive.

The diner bites into the tiny bird whole. It is a religious experience. The rich flesh is said to represent God, the bitter guts the suffering of Jesus, and as the bones of the bird cut into the gums the juices mingle with the diner's own blood, which is said to symbolise the Holy Spirit. The meal is both shameful and exquisite at once, like a really good whore.

But as we ate our *ortolan* that Tuesday, I felt there was something missing, that matters could be improved. The brandy bloody birdy atrocity was losing its thrill.

So. I asked the chef to create for us a special dish that I had been long devising in the experimental kitchen of my mind : *ortalan à l'oie à la mode ultraviolence.* Under my instruction, that restaurant's great chef, Raymond, drowned and *flambéed* half a dozen *ortolans.* He inserted them into a live goose with a flat wooden paddle. Then we began to punch the goose in the face.

"That's a Spicy Fireball !"

The violent struggle of the creature as it was filled with the flaming songbirds, while simultaneously trying to dodge the blows rained upon it by me and my colleagues, produced a rush of feelings in the goose that rendered its flesh divinely tender. Or so I would imagine : I received a nasty nip from the terrified main course and had to retire to the laboratory for treatment and so did not get to taste it. In any event, the waiters refused to serve our party, and went on strike in protest at the fact that the goose had not had a proper holiday before meeting its maker.

Back in the lab, I mused over the events of that day with a glass of Absinthe. I fell into a *rêverie*, thinking of the trinity of flesh, guts and blood ; of Father, Son & Holy Ghost ; of the tripartite motto of *La Belle France—liberté, égalité, fraternité*. I thought of my superb updating of the *ortalan* dish and the ecstasy of innovation, of the admirable refusal of the waiters to allow the goose's labour rights to be breached, of the thrill of setting one's lunch on fire and punching it in the bill.

La modernité ! La grève ! Le déjeuner !

—

The Modernity. The Strikes. The Lunch.

From this, everything flowed. The Centre for Working Luncheon Studies had a purpose, a creed, a *raison d'être*. Our output became prolific, as more and more wonderful innovations were born and gifted to the world. By the time I was halfway through the bottle of Absinthe, I had invented off-shoring—a brilliant piece of financial cleverness whereby one keeps all one's money in a small fishing boat. Three-quarters of the way down, I had developed loutsourcing, whereby the Englishman who wishes for cheap labour can scoop Scottishmen up off the train at your King's Cross station and put them to work right away—after they have been checked for symptoms of *la rage* and had their McEwan's Export confiscated, of course. (France, having no louts of her own, must look on only in envy.)

Finishing the bottle, I left the laboratory and walked the streets, until I invented market research—the useful tool where one wanders around *Les Halles* asking people where the best cheese is kept. As consciousness drained away from me in an especially comfortable gutter, I felt that I had done quite enough brilliant work for one day, or even one lifetime, and resolved to go on strike so as to leave something for future generations to discover. I have been picketing my own office ever since and, if the occasion demands, I shall burn a sheep outside it to make my point and/or a tasty meal.

"Voulez-vous Rioter avec Moi ce Soir ?"

"YOU SAY TOMATO, I SAY TOMATE, YOU SAY POTATO, I SAY POMME DE TERRE, LET'S CALL THE WHOLE THING OEUF"

—TRADITIONAL BRETON WAR CRY

ACROSS THE CHANNEL you do not like to spend too much of the leisure time considering what we Continentals are getting up to, other than to cast envious glances towards our prodigious prowess in the bedroom or gasp in alarm as we peddle our velocipedes through the *Jardins de Luxembourg* with an *élan* of which you can only dream.

However, while it may seem *une proposition scandaleuse* to my many English friends, the time has now come to admit that there is much to learn from the Continent. Some of the great European countries are the coming men of commerce and industry and—currently unparalleled though the might of her Empire may be—Britain ought to take notice of developments from Portugal to Prussia.

The writing, *mes amis*, is on the walls.

Considerable attention must be paid to the nascent Germany, where the aging Von Bismarck has grown bitter and brooding since losing his struggle of power with Kaiser Wilhelm II. Obsessed with his legacy and the identity of the German Empire, the former

FIG. 1. ANY PORK IN A STORM :
THE "SOUTH SEELAND BUBBLE" OR "BUN FIGHT" OF 1878.

The market is flooded with worthless *Wienerchnitzel*
as investors dump the EURO-BAP and clamour for a
return to the Bacon Butty Standard.

Chancellor has become convinced that the traditional German sausage represents all that is great about the Teutonic peoples, and is the vehicle by which the nation can expand.

Now almost entirely mad, he gathers his last remaining physical and political might in a crusade to have the Saveloy introduced as a single currency across Europe. On his most fevered days, Von Bismarck rants that he will not rest until the EUROPEAN SINGLE SAVELOY has been floated against, and then subsumed, the British Pork Scratching and crushed the noble French Saucisson under the heel of its sausagey jackboot.

His three-volume treatise on the subject, *Franc Und Beans*, makes for alarming reading. Even if the battle for supremacy in European finance is fought not in sausages but in currency, it is clear that Germany will have a major part to play, that it most likely will not be pretty to watch, and that cured meats will be involved somehow.

Defeated in the Franco-Prussian war, we in France now lick our wounds and debate whether to toady up to the new Germany or denounce her. Many sage heads in my home country urge the building of an alternate power bloc among the southern European countries, and the coming years may see France attempting to woo them by encouraging a continent-wide EUROPEAN SLEEPING TIME DIRECTIVE. Paris ultimately seeks to align the two-hour French lunch with the Spanish three-hour siesta and the Italian four-hour sit-down in a unified UNIT OF LOAFING. That will have serious implications for the industrious folk of northern Europe, and it may be that future generations of Scottish farmers must begin their day at three in the morning in order to fall in line with the more *laissez-faire* approach to time-keeping further south.

Welcome to the Europe, *mes amis* !

"THE REVOLUTION WILL NOT BE DISORGANISED"

—TRADITIONAL CAMARGUE TEA TOWEL

ALTHOUGH THE BENEFITS of the time-honoured Pyramid structure have been self-evident since ancient times (easy availability of forced labour, compliant slave girls, gold knick-knacks), my colleague Dr Dupont-Neuf's experiments with cooking tobacco and quantum truffles have proven that several alternative organisational structures are theoretically possible :

I. THE 'FLAT' OR STRICTLY HORIZONTAL MANAGEMENT STRUCTURE

WORKING "FLAT OUT" OR "SLEEPING ONE'S WAY TO THE TOP"

II. The 'Top Down' Approach

III. The 'Bottoms Up' Approach

IV. The 'Kill-Bot' Approach

"YOUR CALLING CARD IS IMPORTANT TO US"

—TRADITIONAL NIÇOIS CUSTOMER GREETING

Y OU ENGLISH have your funny pompous attitude to the questions of the heart, but we in France know that in *l'amour*, as in business, too many questions can be a bad thing.

Just as one does not respond to one's wife when she asks about the rouge upon one's collar, sometimes it is essential to dodge a customer enquiry or complaint as if it was a flying crockery.

Taking a system initially pioneered by Parisian waiters, my colleagues Dr Hashkey and Dr Starkey have developed a solution for pretending to listen to the customer while in fact doing nothing at all. I present on their behalf the Completely Automated Letter Listener, Customer Enquiry Nullification & Temporal Reversion Engine, or C. A. L. L. C. E. N. T. R. E.

Fig. 1. *Press* "1" *for impalement,*
Press "2" *for despair.*

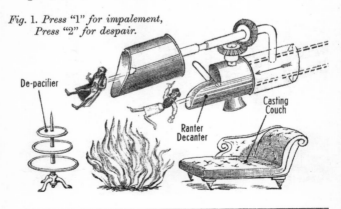

De-pacifier

Ranter Decanter

Casting Couch

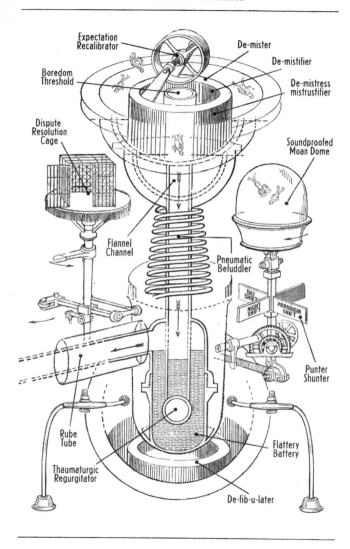

Expectation
Recalibrator

De-mister

De-mistifier

Boredom
Threshold

De-mistress
mistrustifier

Dispute
Resolution
Cage

Soundproofed
Moan Dome

Flannel
Channel

Pneumatic
Befuddler

DAY
SHIFT

NIGHT
SHIFT

PARADIGM
SHIFT

Punter
Shunter

Rube
Tube

Flattery
Battery

Thaumaturgic
Regurgitator

De-fib-u-later

"AT YOUR SERVICE !"

—TRADITIONAL PARISIAN HARLOT

BRITAIN'S COMMERCIAL COLOSSUS has been built upon the sweat and grime of heavy industry and intensive manufacturing : ordinary men, women and children hammering steel with their bare hands, weaving lead ropes until their fingers bleed, mining for cotton (*editor to verify*) and doing whatever else it is that the labouring classes have to do in order to keep themselves in the beer and out of the soup.

The famous saying "Let the working man look after the pennies, and the industrialist will look after the pounds for himself" has been the very expression of the perfect harmony of Britain in the manufacturing age : everyone in his proper place, carrying out his appointed task, and putting his back into it in the shipyard, mine, factory and hair salon.

However, British friends, the future will be quite different. Already the signs are that Britain is moving away from industry in favour of a SERVICE ECONOMY. Where once livings were made in lime and lead, cheap labour means that now even the modest middle-class family can engage at least two maids, plus a house-keeper, gardener, cook, valet, skivvy, hired goon, &c.

If household employ continues to grow at the current rates, by the middle of the next century almost three-quarters of the population will be in domestic service. Napoleon may have referred to the English as a nation of shopkeepers, but increasingly you will be a nation of butlers.

This "Butlerising" of the British employment picture will be excellent news for the writers of melodramas about life in large country houses, as well as providing

PRESENTING ALGERNON AUTOMATON
'THE SILVER SERF'

Serving Suggestion

I CAN'T BELIEVE IT'S NOT BUTLER!

THE WORLD'S FIRST FULLY MECHANICAL MANSERVANT

MAKE WRYLY ARCHED EYEBROWS AND
SIDEWAYS GLANCES A THING OF THE PAST !

WARNING : Keep your Butler-Bot Well Oiled
at all times—Detach 'Below Stairs' Hosing when
Ladies are present—May cause Drowsiness

an alternative to the priesthood for fruity confirmed
bachelors. It will be splendid news for poor women
as well, giving them opportunities to bear a child for
the master of the house and embrace the invigorating
challenge of motherhood after being dismissed from
their posts for getting themselves into trouble. Embrace
the future, working people of Britain : you are all
servants now. The future is ringing the bell, and it is
ready for its brandy and soda. That will be all.

BEING AN EXAMINATION OF
THE SEVEN AND A HALF HABITS
OF HIGHLY EFFECTIVE VICTORIANS

CONJURING MONEY
OUT OF THIN AIR

WITH THE TWENTIETH CENTURY approaching faster
than a speeding bicycle, the old ways of doing
business will soon go the way of underarm bowling,
child labour and the claiming of *droit de seigneur* over
one's prettier scullery maids and under footmen : that
is to say, gone but sorely missed.

In times of yore, a merchant purchased goods and
sold them for profit, or a man in grubby overalls
knocked respectfully at one's tradesman's entrance and
offered to perform services for money. These traditional
methods of economic interaction will presently seem
quite outmoded compared to the trick of producing
money from the clear blue sky.

At the forefront of this modern cleverness is America's
Mr Bernard Madeoff. Thanks to Mr Madeoff's alchemic
ingenuity, the base metal of human folly is transformed
into pure gold. So how does he cultivate a possible
investor ?

"One thing that there's never any shortage of is
rubes," says Mr Madeoff, employing that thrilling
brusque dialect typical of his native Queens (a region
of New York discovered by Her Majesty on a recent

shopping expedition). "And when you get a rube who is greedy as well as stupid, then you're in business.

"You tell the fellow that you've been on a land grab in Africa and that you've got yourself a haul of Tutankhamen's treasure that would take a thousand camels to transport home. You employ an artist to do sketches of the loot, show him the pictures, and then you put on a face as sad as a coyote in a vegetable patch.

"You're in a jam, because you haven't got the money to ship the swag back home, and would he care to invest in bringing back the unimaginable wealth of the ancients, a hundred dollars now to make a thousand in a week's time?"

"If you catch a real live one, you tell him that you'll allow him to sell shares in the expedition to other parties—in exchange for a percentage to ole Madeoff, of course. Soon he's selling to people, and they're selling to people, and they're selling to people, and all along the line you're getting richer than Rockefeller for doing diddly-squat."

Mr Madeoff is certain that within a few years, all business will be conducted in this manner of his pyramid scheme.

"Look at it this way," he says. "Mine here is the perfect commercial model : no stock, no factories, no staff, no repairs, no risk of your competitors inventing a better product and putting you out of business. All you need is the price of a boat passage to Giza, a sketch-artist and your sales patter. Why would anyone choose to do business in the old-fashioned way?"

Sadly, shortly after giving this interview, Mr Madeoff was involved in an unfortunate accident along the Upper Nile when a small pyramid collapsed upon him, giving further credibility to the so-called Curse of Tutankhamen, or the tenacity of the American authorities, depending on your point of view.

BARNUM & BAILOUT'S
MAGNIFICENT
MILLION DOLLAR
MONEY-GO-ROUND

FOR THE BENEFIT OF MR LEHMAN

FANNY MAY
THE BEARDED LADY
HEAR HER BOOM—WATCH HER BUST !

R.B.S. MCKILLOP
THE HUMAN WRECKING BALL

THOSE MAGNIFICENT MEN IN THEIR BANKRUPTCY FILING MACHINES

TOM 'DUMB' THUMB
THE INCREDIBLE SHORT-SELLER

LONDON'S FINEST HIGH-WIRE ARTISTES
THE BIG SWINGING DICKS

—

CHAPTER 6

THINKING OUTSIDE
THE OPERA BOX

BY SIR JOSHUA MONTAGUE-BASHFORTH

—

FORMER VICEROY TO INDIA, LATTERLY GURU

JOSHUA HENRY CHARLES MONTAGUE-BASHFORTH
FIFTH MARQUESS OF SNOOD, KG, GCMG, CBE, IMHO, LOL,
FORMER VICEROY, GOVERNOR GENERAL OF INDIA. GURU.

INDIA. Mysterious. Beguiling. Unseasonably warm. It is a place like almost nowhere else on earth, although it shares a mixture of savagery, strict hierarchy and frequent, eye-watering trips to the lavatory that ought to be familiar to anyone who received his education at one of the major public schools.

I was privileged to spend five years there in the service of Queen and Country, and I learned many lifetimes' worth of splendid and horrible things.

Each day I lived in that country, I stuck to a strict routine : reveille, yoga, shooting a few elephants, a couple of hours on the commode, shooting a native or two, lamb curry, yoga, bed. I became incredibly flexible from the yoga, and as I grew ever more proficient at it, it seemed to me that my very mind expanded as well.

Eventually, my native instructor, Sri Bendatravathan, told me that there was no more he could teach me : I had achieved a state of nirvana. I mastered levitation, walking on hot coals, sleeping on a bed of nails. I made a fortune in competitive-eating contests by eating king prawn phaals without recourse to cucumber raita.

Taking up the name Guru Josh, I wandered the country enlightening the inhabitants. I attempted to convince the Council of India in London that yogic flying would be an excellent technique for the British Army to master, but they could not see my point of view and I regretfully resigned from my post.

Now returned to Britain, I urge any man who wishes to expand his business to first expand his mind. In this chapter, I shall show you how.

Josh

FREE YOUR MIND
AND YOUR ASSETS
WILL FOLLOW

THE POWER OF THE MIND (that is to say, the mind of the right sort of Englishman) is a truly extraordinary thing. Harnessing it is one certain path to success in business.

Clever scientific studies have shown that even the most able men use perhaps just nine per cent of the brain's capacity. And many in the lower ranks of the Constabulary, those involved in the witless puffery of "advertising", and the entire sorry shower who make up the Refuse Collection Department of the London County Council (Islington office), get by well enough on just a minuscule fraction of that.

FIG. 1. MANIAC OR BRANIAC ?

The man who could channel an additional per cent or two of brain matter would find his mind expanded to the degree where almost anything might be possible : extraordinary wealth, wondrous innovation, telepathy, invisibility, even understanding the moods and modalities of the female sex.

A word of caution. However tempting the prospect of an engorged brain may be, do not be fooled by those advertisements in the back of gentlemen's periodicals that offer to increase the size of the body's most important organ. These are the bait of confidence men who seek to sell you nothing more sophisticated than a vacuum pump that will, at best, leave you with a nasty throbbing sensation and, at worst, make you feel even more inadequate than when you started.

The ambitious man who wishes to enlarge his mind ought to begin by meditation. Unfortunately, this can be a devilishly time-consuming business, so many captains of industry are engaging the services of a soulful, lowly paid native fellow to do their meditating for them.

If one lacks the means with which to employ a full-time meditator, one may achieve karmic peace off one's own bat by locking the study door for a few hours each day and focusing the mind. Many find it helpful to listen to a ringing bell, although the disadvantage of this is that one's butler may think one has summoned him to produce the pre-prandial snifter.

Concentrate. Breathe deeply. Imagine the sound of one hand stuffing fistfuls of pound notes into a pocket. Free yourself and let go.

You have now achieved the trance-like state from which all the greatest innovations in commerce and finance were born. The locomotive engine, the five-year government gilt-edged bond, the salted peanut—all of these were dreamed up by great men during meditation.

There is a school of thought that believes two expanded heads are better than one. Consider inviting colleagues to join in these sessions of transcendent contemplation. When several come together to think as one, there may be a meeting of the minds known to advanced business gurus as a BRAIN STORM. Take shelter from one of these ; a deluge of awful ideas may rain down upon you.

C.
CREATING
clouded
judgement

B.
MINGLING
with air
from steamy
secretary

D.
NOTIONS
slowly
crystallise

A.
HOT AIR
rises rapidly
from
manager

E.
AND fall into
a stream of
consciousness

F.
ALLOWING
multiple ideas
to be floated
past colleagues

G.
AND so generate
further brain waves

H.
BEFORE
final siphoning
through the
brain drain

FIG. 2. THE FORMATION OF A BRAIN STORM
OR HOW THE PRINCIPLES OF FROWNIAN MOTION AND DAMP
LADIES MAY COMBINE TO PUT IDEAS INTO ONE'S HEAD

For the novice, better instead to allow one's mind to wander in solitude, perhaps aided by musical performance : this may be termed THINKING OUTSIDE THE OPERA BOX. Let no avenue of mental enquiry be closed to you : if you should find yourself ruminating for some hours as to what Madame Butterfly might look like in her *déshabillé*, or whether you can make a bold break for freedom during the sixth interval of one of the more punishing Germanic masterpieces, indulge your mind. Future generations may be grateful you did.

Consider the inspirational effects of the natural world upon creativity. Forsake the office for an afternoon to enjoy some BLUE SKY THINKING outdoors, perhaps by lying in a punt with a fragrant young companion. Those without access to a punt or a fragrant young companion can achieve similar effects through the consumption of a lot of ale and a nice lie-down on a park bench. Do not underestimate the power of this BROWN ALE THINKING in the generation of clever schemes ; but beware that excessive reliance on the method leads to RED NOSE THINKING, where one becomes easily angered by pigeons or tries to borrow money from strangers for a cup of tea.

By the same regard one should take time to stop and smell the roses, and not be frightened by the prospect of thinking about more than one problem at a time ; the cross-pollination of ideas can often be highly effective, especially if they can be hothoused via the FLOWER POWER of POSITIVE THINKING. Imagine yourself to be the gardener of your own mind's garden, and do not be afraid to spread a lot of manure around in order to grow an idea from seed.

As you seek to become wealthy through mind expansion and contemplation, remember above all that there are no incorrect ideas, although there may well be some indecent ones. Free your mind, and your bottom line will follow.

ENVISIONING THE FUTURE OF YOUR ENTERPRISE

Dear reader, join me in picturing some of mankind's most arresting accomplishments. The Great Pyramid at Giza. The Great Western Railway. The Great Britain women's hockey team in their Christmas charity calendar (adults-only limited edition).

Like any other remarkable undertaking, they were all once no more than sparks of inspiration in a man of foresight, a man who dared to dream. Ask yourself : what is my vision for my business ?

It may help to go into a trance-like state—with the use of opiates or an especially good lunch if need be—as you attempt to envisage how your enterprise would exist in the future. If your budget allows, consider engaging the services of a soothsayer or seer to aid you in this ; at the very least you should be able to undertake a little home augury on the boardroom table with a pigeon or two.

Free your mind ; imagine what it is that you want to achieve. Write it down before the enlightened state fades or it is time for dinner.

You are now ready for the next critical staging post on your journey to business nirvana : writing your Statement Of Committed Corporate Intent Relaying Motives Of Missionary Zeal. The useful mnemonic acronym SOCCIRMOMZ is here your friend. The SOCCIRMOMZ is a short description of your company's ethos, beliefs, activities and goals. If that seems daunting, see for inspiration some of the following mission statements :

WE AIM TO PROVIDE SOLUTIONS TO CUSTOMER LEAD PROBLEMS

—

Packnough & Sons Industrial Chemicals,
who specialise in creating water-based acids so
powerful that they can burn through lead, and
sometimes customers as well.

OUR AMBITION IS TO RAISE STANDARDS BY STRATEGIC CLIENT-FACING CAMPAIGNS

—

Regimental motto of the
Northumberland Colonial Dragoons,
who have successfully intervened in clients' faces
in a series of campaigns from the Sudan to
South Africa and raised their standard in many
a hot and beastly foreign clime.

ATTEMPTING TO CULTIVATE REWARDING NEW RELATIONSHIPS AND DISPLAY DYNAMIC PERFORMANCE WITH A GOAL OF TOTAL CUSTOMER SATISFACTION

—

"Strumpet Sue" of Covent Garden,
voted "Best Value Tart" at last year's
Fallen Women in Business Awards.

As you can see, a mission statement need not make
sense or carry any meaning per se. The important
factor is that it should sound impressive and give you
something to put on letterheads &c. Now it is only a
matter of working out how you will spend all the money.

THE HINDOO MANAGER : ORGANISATIONAL THEORY AND THE UNIVERSAL CONSCIOUSNESS

DURING MY TIME IN INDIA I was greatly impressed by Hindoo-ism, and it struck me that it would be an excellent model for the modern commercial enterprise. Now, I should stress that my understanding of this ancient religion comes almost entirely from conversations I had with my barber, Mr Ganguly. Ganguly was a capital fellow with the badger-hair brush and thinning scissors, but an incurable dipsomaniac, gambler and ranter, so his theological insights might be as haphazard as his haircuts after he'd had a big wager come home in one of the native grasshopper-fighting tournaments.

That said, I am a remorselessly hirsute individual and the hot climate of Calcutta necessitated I have my hair cut at least once a day in order to maintain the smart appearance that is essential for a Senior British Officer in any foreign outpost. Therefore I certainly had a huge quantity of religious insight, even if its quality was dubious. As good old Ganguly snipped and lathered away at my hair and moustaches, he would explain to me about the Hindoo set-up ; and a jolly fine one it sounds, too.

Your Hindoo is of the belief in a Brahman, a Godhead who is at once what one might call the top man on the island, as well as some species of universal energy who flows through all entities. As Ganguly explained this, it occurred to me right away that this is exactly how

FIG 1. BRAVO BRAHMAN !
THE SO-CALLED "MAMMOTH OF MAMMON" AND
WORLD'S FIRST MULTI-TASKING MULTI-TUSKER

FIG 2. *"Is that a piece of the Godhead in your pocket or are you just pleased to see me ?"*

a really first-rate Chairman runs a business. He is a supremely powerful figurehead who is also involved in the minutiæ of every aspect from production to sales to covering up the exact number of workers who have dropped off their perches from factory-inspired respiratory difficulties.

Underneath the Brahman sit strata of deities or Devas, celestial beings who control aspects of existence such as the wind, war, love, cheese and so on. These are analogous to the heads of department in a large well-run organisation, each responsible for his own area but really just an aspect or arm of the Chairman Godhead himself. Good eggs, the lot of them.

Now that I have retired from lording it over Indians to run my own wool factory in Preston, I try to behave at all times like a supernatural omniscient being whose energy flows through all things like a drop of water in an infinite pool. And once my research laboratory has made good on my instructions to attach an extra two pairs of arms to my torso, I am sure day-to-day operations will run even more smoothly.

ENLIGHTENED

DIVINE SH'MO
OR CHAIRMAN
*Supreme Being
& all-round
Good Egg*

PARTLY
ENLIGHTENED

UNDA
SH'MO

BO'HO SH'MO
*Being a bearded
wünderkind*

*Wheel of karmic
promotions &
demotions*

BAD'ASS
SH'MO'FO'
*Being a cosmic
force to be
reckoned with*

FAUX SH'MO
Being a less-than-celestial manager

COMPLETELY
IN THE DARK

SH'MUK
*Being a sh'mo re-born
as a BEAN COUNTER*

UDDA
SH'MUK
*Being a sh'mo
re-born as a BEAN*

FIG 3. THE SMARTER STRATA.
INTELLIGENT APPLICATION OF THE PRINCIPLES OF
PERPETUAL REINCARNATION ENSURES STAFF TURNOVER
IS KEPT TO A MINIMUM

THE CREATIVE ENVIRONMENT

FOR THOSE OF US wielding shovels at the coalface of managerial imagineering, the need for a refuge from the distractions of daily life is self-evident. The creative mind thrives more fully in creative surroundings, enriched by inspiring artefacts and imposing architecture.

My own family needed little persuading of the benefits of secluded thought and on my return home from India my uncle immediately ordered a special thinking chamber to be built for me in his attic. I must confess that his design differs from mine in a few respects—while I appreciate the addition of cushioned walls for bouncing ideas off, I do find myself lamenting the absence of windows—but that being said, safely tucked up in my triple-buckled pajamas, I do at last feel my mind wandering entirely free.

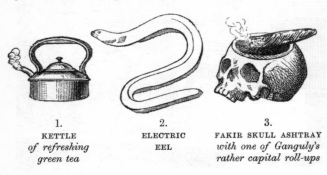

1.	2.	3.
KETTLE	ELECTRIC	FAKIR SKULL ASHTRAY
of refreshing	EEL	*with one of Ganguly's*
green tea		*rather capital roll-ups*

FIG. 1. STIMULATING OBJECTS

A—Close drapes
B—Inhale deeply
C—Await arrival
   of Talking Fox

FIG. 2. A ROOM WITH A (SOMEWHAT ENHANCED) VIEW

BEING AN EXAMINATION OF
THE SEVEN AND A HALF HABITS
OF HIGHLY EFFECTIVE VICTORIANS

No 6

ATTEMPTING FREQUENT FEATS OF SEAFARING OR AERONAUTICAL DAREDEVILRY

WHEN A MAN HAS MADE A GREAT DEAL OF MONEY, two traditional courses of action are open to him. He may follow the example of great Americans such as oil's Rockefeller, banking's Morgan and pretend-chicken's Roosterbender, raising his bat to the crowd and remarking his guard with a mind to making even more money in the afternoon session. Or he may take his lead from our own Peabody and Booth, or even from Master Jas. Oliver's marvellous initiatives to get the poor and ignorant using their knives and forks correctly at table, and set his mind to "giving something back" to the needy.

Yet there may be a third way emerging, and right in the vanguard of this new approach to wealth is Baron Raechard von Bransaün, founder and Chairman of Jungfrau and Sons Ltd. Von Bransaün made his first fortune selling sheet music at an aggressive discount, and moved on to publishing the musical compositions of others, notably the hypnotic dirge for brass and campanologist "Tuba Bells" and its even more aurally demanding successor, the politically provocative Irish Potato Famine-inspired ballad "Tuber O'Balls". Despite subsequent persistent attempts to lose money with ventures as diverse and disastrous as railways and syrupy drinks, Baron von Bransaün continues only to become wealthier and wealthier.

"It is true, I cannot get rid of this money for the life of me," he says. "More and more of it persists in finding its way into my bank account, and I have grown so tired of this. I am finding the world of business to be rather boring these days and have instead decided to dedicate the rest of my life and fortune to feats of speed and exhilaration."

IN THE DRINK

IN THE PURSUIT OF EXCITEMENT, the Baron has already tried to navigate across the Channel to France in a copper bath, a bid whose audaciousness was only partly undermined by his needing to be rescued by the Coastguard in Dover.

"I was undeterred," says the Baron. "Indeed, it made me only more convinced that I should one day achieve maritime greatness. I hastened overland to Cadiz, where I undertook a voyage to sail around the tip of Spain and up into the Straits of Gibraltar in a child's shoe with Jungfrau and Sons Ltd painted on the side.

"It is true that I had to be fished out of the drink in Cadiz Harbour by *El Armada Española*, but once I had calmed *El Capitan* down with some soothing words and offers of free second-class tickets on my London to Manchester railway, everybody got on quite famously.

"Until the Naval officers had to go on my trains, that is," laughs the Baron. "I did have a telegram from a Rear-Admiral saying that he wished he'd left me in the water, but then that of course is the famous Spanish sense of humour."

Now barred from every port in Europe, the Baron has begun to focus his full energies on an even greater frontier : SPACE.

"I am planning to sail to Mars in a Balloon powered by my own brand of unspecified spirit-based alcoholic drink," says the Baron. "It will be my most triumphant voyage yet, and I am pleased to report that almost everybody I have spoken to has said, 'Yes, yes, please, please, please try to fly to Mars in a wicker basket.' One friend even remarked that it was a 'win-win scenario', but I am unfamiliar with this idiom so I just shook his hand and smiled for the photographic plate."

Remember : business can be rather boring, but attempting to drown yourself in an ill-advised nautical stunt or defy the laws of gravity and reason is never without thrills, and can provide invaluable publicity, as well as giving the emergency services something to do.

CHAPTER 7

HUMILITY·SERVICE· REGULAR BUFFING

THE WHOLE MAN

BY DALE CARNEGIE-HALL

—

VISITING FELLOW OF MANLY HANDSHAKES
ALL SOULS' COLLEGE, DROITWICH

GIN & TONIC ALLEY :
SIMILAR TO GIN LANE BUT WITH NICER SHOES

IF YOU HAVE FOLLOWED the instructions of the esteemed experts in this book's preceding six chapters, you ought now to be well on the path to being a very important man indeed. But the race is not won. Indeed, the life of the rich man is considerably more demanding and complicated than that of the poor.

The poor man has only one worry : getting enough food to give him sufficient energy to work himself to death in order to stay alive and put food on the table. How I envy the noble simplicity of his toil, for the rich man has no such freedom.

He must divine for himself not only how to allocate his time between work and leisure but how to spend his wealth meaningfully and responsibly. For with great power come a great deal of annoying little people asking you for money, and their demands on your time are constant.

It may seem to you that money opens a panoply of possibilities, but not even the most cruel dictator or overseer—with the notable exception of Thos. Postlethwaite, the notoriously hard-line wool and wooden-leg baron of Warrington—is more tyrannical than unfettered choice. This chapter will be your guide as you work out what to do with your newfound wealth and free time.

Dale

JUGGLING WORK + FAMILY*

IT IS SAID that one of the great socio-economic challenges of the age is that of achieving a balance between life and work. How true. The need to get work done versus the risk of employees losing their lives is indeed a delicate equation.

For those fortunate to be employed in posts where fatalities are rare, other questions arise. How much work constitutes too much ? Ought the lower orders to be allowed one half-day's leisure time each month ? Or is this a slippery slope towards Continental-style idling and licentious daydreaming ? And what of the modern phenomenon of so-called "personal injury lawyers" : ought factory owners to pursue legal action against workers who get blood, severed limbs, &c. on the shop floor ? Everywhere, the rules of the workplace are in flux.

For instance, the prevailing tendency towards namby-pambyism now sees Englishmen clamouring to spend more time with their progeny rather than less. In previous generations, a gentleman saw a child at its Christening, on the eve of its departure for boarding school, and then again on its twenty-first birthday. Even so, the more emotionally unyielding man conducted these meetings from behind a screen in the study to prevent a child from becoming clingy.

These days, one hears of men placing portable photographic plates of their children on their desks. Some even send a carrier pigeon home at lunch-time with billing and cooing messages to their issue. This is the way of the world now and, as Mr Darwin has observed, we must adapt or die : separating work and home is, regrettably, impossible.

---

* Non-circus-based applications

*Note to self : Always remember to lock away the matches
on "Bring Your Child to Work Day"*

How to "fit in" with the child-pandering mood *du jour*,
then ? If there is no suitable *photolumière* practitioner in
your locality, take the children themselves to your office
and arrange them in a cabinet. Entreat your firm to
implement a "Bring Your Children To Work" scheme.
Be it book-keeping, coal-mining, asbestos-blowing,
asbestos-sucking, cattle-rustling or knife-fighting, any
lad will relish the chance to see how the paterfamilias
provides. Better yet, lobby for a "Bring Your Children
To Work—To Work" programme, in which you compel
the boy to do your work while you have yourself a well-
earned rest and perhaps a glass of something refreshing.
After all, what is the point of having children if they
do not make one's lot in life more comfortable ?

EMPLOYEE RELATIONS (FOR THOSE NOT EMPLOYING RELATIONS)

WHERE POSSIBLE, always engage the services of a relative. Family members settle for smaller salaries, especially youngsters who have yet to grasp the value of currency. A hearty seventeen-mile walk to the pit or silage depot gives families a chance to spend time together. For those further up the economic ladder, an imbecile cousin can be kept under close supervision in a sinecure posting at your firm ; accounts payable is an ideal backwater in which to station an idiot relative. And in the spirit of "The family that works together stays together", any workplace difficulties can be solved agreeably over the humble family supper, or with violence on the way to Evensong.

Of course, it may not be feasible to hire blood relatives. It may be that your family members are lazy. You may be an orphan. Perhaps you have had to flee Great Britain after a shameful incident involving a domestic servant and an incorrectly tuned pianola, settling instead in the liberating anonymity of the Argentine pampas, building up a formidable canned meat empire and relying for support solely on your trusted retainer, Diego.

If your staff are non-relations, you have two options to keep them satisfied. You can pay them a fair wage ; or, more realistically, bamboozle them with biannual bagatelles and bonhomie at a) Yuletide and b) The Summer Company Pick-Nick.

All that is needed at Christmas is some plum duff, facility for the sillier employees to make brass rubbings

*Sir William Gutteridge, Fridge Magnate, rides his team
to victory at the annual employee Sports Day*

of their fundaments and a lot of gin. Summer festivities
require more planning, and should feature athletic
competitions of the Sports Day stripe. Staff who have
lost a limb in industrial misfortunes will enjoy the one-
legged race, while hungrier, lowly paid employees will
find the potato and spoon contest a source of delight
as well as some welcome nutrition. All are sure to
relish a flunky-plutocrat piggyback race, and a few
modest prizes—a cup of cider, rudimentary medical
treatment—will ensure that a good time is had by
winner and loser alike.

The important thing to remember is that everyone
should have fun in an informal setting, although do feel
free to terminate the employment of anyone who bests
you on the sports field.

THERE IS NO "ME" IN "PHILANTHROPY"

HOW THEN, is the rich man to "give something back" to society ? I shall tell you.

Find a deprivation or need that engenders a stirring in your breast. It may be the matter of hungry urchins. It may be the need to provide for the elderly and hopelessly decrepit. It may be a want of acceptable golf clubs in your county. Identify the cause that inspires you, and throw yourself into improving the situation.

I myself have a particular calling for picking up fallen women, and devote considerable amounts of my energies to The Dale Carnegie-Hall Correctional Facility for Girls Who Have Been Wicked but May yet be Saved from Themselves with the Application of the Firm but Loving Hand of a Kindly Old Uncle. Painting the letters for the sign alone took me several weeks, but the philanthropist does not allow himself to be disheartened by hard work, and thinks instead of all those wicked young women whom he may be able to help, to say nothing of the tax advantages.

It is true that I have yet to attract any applications from girls who have got themselves into Trouble. Furthermore, the police have started to show some interest in my little institute, turning up rudely and unannounced to ask quite forward questions about my entirely blameless motives. One detective inspector even went so far as to accuse me of knowing something about those awful murders in the East End in the late 1880s. But did not our Lord himself find considerable resistance to his message of kindness and unconditional love ? I believe that if Christ Himself were on Earth today,

FIG. 1. EASY VIRTUE IS ITS OWN REWARD

He would be alongside me in Whitechapel handing out notices to women of easy virtue and inviting them to come and stay for the weekend, no questions asked.

The ingratitude (often violent) of those one is trying to help is a sad fact of life for the philanthropist, who ought to be under no illusion about just how hard a fallen woman can kick when cornered. With that in mind, I have begun to turn my attention to bestowing my bounty upon the *hoi polloi* in other ways.

Impressed by the fine work my friend Sir Ebenezer Howard has done with his Garden City project, I have similarly been working on a dream urban development that may shape the future for our country. I exhibited my plan for Daletown at the 1896 World's Fair (East Midlands Section) and was gratified by the audible gasps from my audience.

At considerable expense, I engaged the services of town planners, architects and clairvoyants to help me design a town that will provide future residents with a glorious, spacious new way of life. Daletown's central feature is a very large cathedral whose nave is modelled on the shape of my own cranium—my one little concession to vanity. Shops, houses and factories are arranged like the petals of a rose around Saint Dale's, and I intend to encourage the residents of neighbouring, overcrowded Kidderminster to relocate to Daletown with the promise of affordable houses, jobs in one of the factories doing something or other, and free copies of my book *How to Design a Cathedral along the Lines of your Own Head and Influence People*.

Even the scale model itself was a thing of some beauty, although it is sadly no more. The project ran into some financial choppy waters after I encouraged 10,000 carpet workers to leave Kidderminster for a better life in Daletown. Unfortunately, many of them arrived before work on housing &c. had finished, or in fact begun, and I had no option but to house them in the scale-model version. It is a sad reflection on the innate ingratitude of the working class that they found living 500 to a room in terraced houses the size of a teacup beneath their station, and the model was unconscionably reduced to matchwood.

All things considered, I think it might be easier and simpler to set up a donkey sanctuary and have done with it.

BETTER LIVING THROUGH WORKING JOLLY HARD

WORK PROVIDES THE COMMON MAN, woman or child with many opportunities for personal ennoblement. Consult this handy chart representing the DIGNITY OF LABOUR to see where your employ ranks on the recognised moral hierarchy of recompensed endeavour.

PHILANTHROPIST
AND AUTHOR

—

QUEEN
MISSIONARY
FLORENCE NIGHTINGALE
AMATEUR CRICKETER
VICAR
PROFESSIONAL CRICKETER

SERVANT
ROBBING THE POOR, WEAK, ORPHANED, &C.
THE LAW (AS ABOVE)
FLOOZIE
MURDERER
THE STAGE
CHILD MURDERER
BEING A NOISY OR DISRESPECTFUL CHILD

THE DESPICABLE PRACTICES OF ADVERTISING & MARKETING
REGICIDE
PROFESSIONAL FRENCHMAN

JOURNALISM, POPULAR

BEING AN EXAMINATION OF
THE SEVEN AND A HALF HABITS
OF HIGHLY EFFECTIVE VICTORIANS

MAINTAINING A STRICT SEPARATION BETWEEN PRIVATE AND PUBLIC LIVES

OUR SEVENTH TITAN OF INDUSTRY overcame enormous personal disadvantages (including but not limited to being born in Australia) to rise to pre-eminence in his chosen field. His longevity, ferocity and relentless acquisition of younger wives are legendary. He has transformed the newspaper from being a medium of information into a species of popular entertainment, in addition to being a reliable source of salacious etchings of young females. He owns over one hundred newspapers across the world and frequently visits each one to keep morale high, or horsewhip employees as need be. At the age of eighty-seven, he personally settled a labour dispute with a bare-knuckle boxing bout. For many years, he used the former Prime Minister, Lord Russell, as a toast rack. Dear reader : he knows precisely what sort of activities you were engaged in last summer.

He is, it hardly needs saying, the brilliant publisher Mr Rhubarb Guttersby-Snoop.

Born in abject Australianism in 1795, Rhubarb—so named because of his childhood fondness for attacking other children with sticks of the toothsome yet offensively shaped fruit—displayed an inquisitive and aggressive nature from a very early age. By the age of six, he was the proprietor of his small town's newspaper, the *Woolloongabba Examiner*. By eight he had masterminded a hostile takeover of its fierce rival, the *Woolloongabba Sentinel* (incorporating *Dingo Monthly*).

By the time he reached manhood's estate, he had a media empire that was beginning to stretch across the globe. A fondness for foreign travel and a horror of income tax encouraged him to embark upon a peripatetic lifestyle that sees him rarely spend more than a few days in any country, staying just long enough to take control of its major publications and have his long-time majordomo, Ginger, rustle as many police horses as the pair can reasonably fit on their private schooner.

TUNE IN, TURN ON, TON UP

Now a sprightly one-hundred-and-one, Rhubarb attributes his continued success to one golden rule.

"Always remember the distinction between the private life and the public," he says. "Find out what people want to keep private, and then make it as public as possible. That's where the money lies."

Rhubarb elucidates. "Go public with the fact that it is in your private interest to keep the public informed of matters that others consider private.

"You would be quite amazed how much you can find out if you know where to look, and just how helpful people can be to you once you have taken a close personal interest in their affairs."

Employing a network of rooters, rustlers, ferreters, scavengers, bin-dippers, eavesdroppers and trusted public servants, Rhubarb has made it his life's work to know everything there is to know about all the major public figures of our age, and many private ones as well. This has at times brought him into conflict with the authorities, but again and again they have been persuaded to listen to reason in exchange for the enduring support of Rhubarb's more vigorous organs.

Indeed, the Earl of Aberdeen attributed his 1852 General Election victory solely to the backing of Rhubarb's *Sunday Morning Evening Bugle*, whose famous headline "It Might Well Have Been the *Sunday Morning Evening Bugle* What Could Be Said To Have (In Part) Engendered This Recent Success of the Earl of Aberdeen's Peelite Faction" reflected the significance of Rhubarb's patronage.

And it has also been said that the slogan "Will the last person to leave Great Britain kindly extinguish the candles, tell Sarah-Jane she might turn in early and have a quick tot of port before putting the dog and the chimney-sweep's boy out for the night ?" was a decisive blow in the defeat of Viscount Melbourne's Whigs back in the 'thirties. Similarly, a series of "embrace-and-unburden" feature articles in Rhubarb's publications— where a string of disreputable ladies came forward to attest to Melbourne's hands-on approach to domestic corporal punishment—also played their part.

To conclude, it is not what you know, it is who knows what about you, and nobody knows more about anybody else than brave, noble, wise and munificent Rhubarb.

LAST ORDERS

BY QUEEN MARY OF SCHOPPS

—

DEPUTY DUCHESS OF LOWER SAXONY

QUEEN MARY OFFERS SOME FRIENDLY ADVICE
TO A LOCAL SHOPKEEPER

WINDOW DRESS
FOR SUCCESS

REVIEWING, RETELLING, RETAILING AND PUNISHING
PEOPLE WHO HAVE NOT BEEN CONCENTRATING

IF YOU HAVE STUDIED this book assiduously, you will
now possess a formidable arsenal of techniques with
which to conquer the world of industry.

I myself have fought and won battles in my own
chosen arena : the gladiatorial world of retail. As
a young woman, I would survey the high street in
Rickmansworth with its querulous haberdashers and
lackadaisical milliners and my blood would boil. I
vowed that I would make each and every one of these
enterprises more profitable, more enticing and more
expertly managed. I strode up to the door of a dowdy
upholsterer and knocked upon it. I persuaded him to
let me rearrange his window display. He was unsure
about the new look. I offered to rearrange his features
instead. He declared himself delighted with the results.

I cut a swathe through that high street like a modern-
day Attila the Hun, albeit with a better eye for
product placement and brightening up a shop window.
Cheesemongers, druggists, silkmen, cobblers : soon
all had fallen to my bow and arrow and I had made
Rickmansworth a hub of exquisitely well-decorated
emporia. Behind every successful shopkeeper is a woman

shouting suggestions and directions at him, and for you to become that woman, all you must do is this : find the right questions to ask, and do not take no for an answer.

Ask yourself : what is my goal in business ? Is it expansion ? Increased profits ? To dance on the grave of my vanquished rivals ? To take over the manufacturing infrastructure of an entire continent ? To scrape together enough of a dowry to prise a homely daughter off the Chesterfield and into a bridal gown ? Or is it simply to make sure that every employee is wearing the right sort of hat ?

Whatsoever your desire might be, break each business situation down into its component parts, in the same way that you would break the spirit of a slovenly shop girl. Address each in turn, precisely, clearly and with utter conviction, as if it were a member of the lower orders or a foreigner, and then act swiftly and decisively.

You must learn quickly that delegation is important, and therefore surround yourself only with individuals of the highest calibre. To this end, insist that any prospective employee takes and passes my Mastery of Business Administering examination paper, a sample of which is provided later in this chapter. The Diploma is recognised wherever English is spoken, or at least in places which ascribe credibility to postal diplomas. For an additional fee, examination candidates who fail to achieve the required standards receive a personal visit from me at their business premises for the talking-to of their life.

No matter how well run any business is, there will always be pitfalls along the way. There is no shame in asking for help, if you have the means to pay for it. Do feel free to make an enquiry at one of my own personal commercial clinics : apply at the Houses of Parliament and ask for Mary.

Trouble-shooting—not to be confused with troublemaker-shooting—has enabled me to rescue and rehabilitate failing operations from a struggling dual-purpose abattoir and perfumery in Cologne to a decrepit fleet of horse-drawn carriages in the Elbe-Weser Triangle, birthplace of mechanically recovered cheese. My satisfied clients in Cologne now have access to a ready supply of horse meat, and while locals in the Elbe-Weser Triangle are now compelled to walk everywhere, they most certainly smell a great deal better than they used to.

As this example demonstrates, it is the ability not just to apply knowledge but to see the larger panorama that is the key to success. It is also important to be able to take a certain—how best to express this ?—a certain relish in making the hard decisions.

There may be tough choices to be made in the future, but with God, clear thinking and a *laissez-faire* approach to employment law on our side, the sturdy vessel of British enterprise will sail into a glorious future of worldwide dominance eternal.

—MARY

MASTERY OF BUSINESS ADMINISTERING

—

EXAMINATION

PAPER A

—

TIME ALLOWED : ONE HOUR
CANDIDATES MAY CONSULT SLIDE RULES & FORMER
GOVERNESSES IN CALCULATING THEIR ANSWERS

---

1 : STAFFING & RECRUITMENT

FOLLOWING a small misunderstanding with the coat check girl at Rumfellows, and the subsequent elopement of said girl with the entire staff of your London office, the position of Under-Assistant Manager has now fallen vacant. Peruse the following candidates and identify the most deserving for the post :

CANDIDATE A
Currently
Head of Customer
Engagement.

CANDIDATE B
Currently
Engaged to
your Niece.

A Clerk quits his bank in the City at 3.00 pm sharp, travelling on foot in a westerly direction at three miles an hour. He carries 26 gold sovereigns in a leather purse with a small hole in the bottom, one sovereign falling to the ground every 300 yds. At precisely 3.15 pm, an overseer leaves his lard factory in Paddington, travelling on crutches in an easterly direction at two miles an hour, the large hole in his left boot obliging him to pause for one minute every half mile to remove any rusty nails, tacks, &c. which are lodged there.

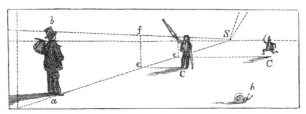

Q—Assuming both parties conform to the values and behaviours one might expect from their relative stations in life, how many minutes must elapse before the Clerk is clubbed to his death by an avaricious crutch-wielding assailant ?

. . . .

How many coins does the malfeasant escape with ?

. . . .

And for an additional mark, which is the nearest police station ?

. . . .

3 : CORPORATE GOVERNANCE

YOU SIT ON THE BOARD of a leading Codswallop manufactory.
The business, founded by your father and uncle, has now
passed to the next generation and is apportioned in the
following manner :

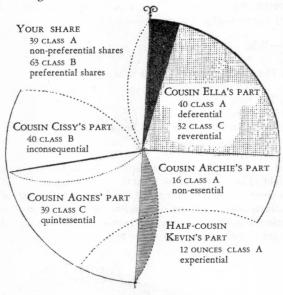

YOUR SHARE
39 CLASS A
non-preferential shares
63 CLASS B
preferential shares

COUSIN ELLA'S PART
40 CLASS A
deferential
32 CLASS C
reverential

COUSIN CISSY'S PART
40 CLASS B
inconsequential

COUSIN ARCHIE'S PART
16 CLASS A
non-essential

COUSIN AGNES' PART
39 CLASS C
quintessential

HALF-COUSIN
KEVIN'S PART
12 OUNCES CLASS A
experiential

Q—Assuming each family member leaves his share to
you, how many cousins have to perish in tragic and entirely
unrelated boating accidents before you are in a position to
assume a controlling interest in the company ?

ANSWER :
A—All of the above
B—Kissing Cousins only
C—Robin Cousins

4 : ACCOUNTING (CREATIVE)

NATHANIEL works for an investment bank that lends money to tribesmen of the Serengeti so that they may purchase terraced houses in Putney. Unfortunately, the tribesmen of the Serengeti have not mastered the concept of compound interest ; nor do they wish to live in Putney. Nathaniel has lost a great deal of money for the bank.

Q—Who is to blame ?

a) The Government for failing to regulate Nathaniel's activities properly
b) The British taxpayer
c) The Greeks, or some such
d) Unforeseeable global forces beyond the sight or control of any reasonable person

For an additional five marks, explain why Nathaniel's bank ought to be bailed out with public funds. Extra credit will be given for demonstrating why regulation is the enemy of business innovation and how terrible it would be for the nation if Nathaniel moved to Frankfurt. Candidate should award himself large bonus at any time.

Send your completed examination paper together with a banker's order for 9/6 to :
Uxbridge Examination Board, Garnons-Williams Campus, Wig Lane, Stamford, Lincs., and
your degree (if eligible) will be awarded by return of post. Strictly no messenger pigeons.

BEING AN EXAMINATION OF
THE SEVEN AND A HALF HABITS
OF HIGHLY EFFECTIVE VICTORIANS

 Nº 7½

NEVER MISS A CHANCE TO FLAUNT YOUR WARES

NOW AVAILABLE FROM ALL GOOD BOOKMONGERS

"Come to Papa"

WHO MOVED MY STILTON ?
THE VICTORIAN GUIDE TO
GETTING AHEAD IN BUSINESS

First published 2012
Bloomsbury Publishing Plc
50 Bedford Square
London WC1B 3DP
www.bloomsbury.com

ISBN 978 1 4088 2432 0

A CIP catalogue record for this book is available from
the British Library.

This book is produced using paper that is made from wood grown in
managed, sustainable forests. It is natural, renewable and recyclable.
The logging and manufacturing processes conform to the
environmental regulations of the country of origin.

10 9 8 7 6 5 4 3 2 1

Typeset in Gin Modern.
Printed and bound in Great Britain by
CPI Group (UK) Ltd, Croydon CR0 4YY